Roots Matter

Roots Matter

Healing History, Honoring Heritage, Renewing Hope

PAULA OWENS PARKER

PICKWICK Publications • Eugene, Oregon

ROOTS MATTER
Healing History, Honoring Heritage, Renewing Hope

Copyright © 2016 Paula Owens Parker. All rights reserved. Except for brief quotations in critical publications or reviews, no part of this book may be reproduced in any manner without prior written permission from the publisher. Write: Permissions, Wipf and Stock Publishers, 199 W. 8th Ave., Suite 3, Eugene, OR 97401.

Pickwick Publications
An Imprint of Wipf and Stock Publishers
199 W. 8th Ave., Suite 3
Eugene, OR 97401

www.wipfandstock.com

PAPERBACK ISBN: 978-1-4982-3060-5
HARDCOVER ISBN: 978-1-4982-3062-9
ELECTRONIC ISBN: 978-1-4982-3061-2

Cataloguing-in-Publication data:

Names: Parker, Paula Owens
Title: Roots matter : healing history, honoring heritage, renewing hope / Paula Owens Parker.
Description: Eugene, OR : Pickwick Publications, 2016. | Includes bibliographical references.
Identifiers: ISBN 9781498230605 (paperback) | ISBN 9781498230629 (hardcover) | ISBN 9781498230612 (ebook)
Subjects: LCSH: African American—Violence against—United States. | African American—Psychology. | Intergenerational relations. | Family assessment. | Reconciliation.
Classification: LCC RC451.5.N4 P19 2016 (print) | LCC RC451.5.N4 (ebook)

Manufactured in the U.S.A.   06/20/2016

For my people standing staring trying to fashion a better way
from confusion, from hypocrisy and misunderstanding,
trying to fashion a world that will hold all the people,
all the faces, all the adams and eves and their countless generations.

MARGARET WALKER

Contents

Acknowledgments | ix
Introduction | xi

Part I: Roots Matter: Healing History, Honoring Heritage, Renewing Hope | 1

Chapter 1
Family Systems, Genogram, and Biblical Examples | 6

Chapter 2
Generational Trauma in Jewish, Armenian, and Native American History | 24

Chapter 3
Generational Trauma in African American History | 42

Chapter 4
Theological Review: Matthew V. Johnson, Flora Keshgegian, Shelly Rambo, Dominic Robinson | 55

Chapter 5
Course Description: Roots Matter: Healing History, Honoring Heritage, Renewing Hope | 71

Chapter 6
Conclusion: Findings, Recommendations, and Further Study | 78

Part II: Roots Matter: Healing History, Honoring Heritage, Renewing Hope—Leader's Guide | 89

Introduction | 91

Session One
Family Systems and the Genogram | 97

Session Two
Old Testament and Family Stories | 109

Session Three
Generational Trauma in Jewish, Armenian,
and Native American History | 121

Session Four
Generational Trauma in African American History | 136

Session Five
Trauma, Mourning, Resilience, and Hope | 148

Session Six
Evaluation and Healing Service | 160

Session Seven
Follow-up Session (optional) | 164

Illustration—Table 1: D/P Class Project Expenses
September 4—October 9, 2012 | 169

Appendix A
Consent Form | 171

Appendix B
Syllabus | 177

Appendix C
Definitions of Different Trauma Types | 182

Appendix D
Program Evaluation | 187

Appendix E
Roots Matter Healing Service | 193

Glossary | 199
Bibliography | 205

Acknowledgments

To Dr. Katie Geneva Cannon, my advisor, whose wisdom, patience, guidance, expertise, steadfast commitment, and consistent affirmation transformed my dreams and visions into this document. To Drs. Gerardo James de Jesus and Matthew V. Johnson, my professors at San Francisco Theological Seminary, whose teaching of the "*imago Dei*" and "tragic vision" became fundamental to this project. To Rev. Mavis Hannah Yeboah, who hosted me when I visited Ghana and walked with me through Elmina and Cape Coast slave castles.

To Jane Camp and Shirley Moore, who introduced me to healing prayer and took me on a spiritual journey that deepened my faith, healed my spirit, and transformed my life. To Sandi and Bob Kerner and Russ Parker, who expanded my understanding of the healing ministry and encouraged me to pursue this work.

To Angela Duncan and Carmen Foster, who called me every day giving me emotional support and advice to keep me focused. To my prayer partners, Rose Marie Edwards, Sandy Gramling, Sandi Kerner, Loucinda McLean, Russ Parker, Robert Sears, Doug Schoeninger, and Fontaine Williamson, who kept all of us in constant prayer during the six-week class time. To class speakers Jan Brown and Sandi Kerner, whose testimonies about their generational healing inspired us all. To class participants, Elnora Allen, Kelle Brown, Willie Dell, Angela Duncan, David Foster, Olivia Foster, Tiffany Hall, Michael Jackson, Elianah Jordan, Lorae Ponder, Consuelo Staton, and Roberta Walker, who trusted me with their time and family stories and gave me invaluable feedback that helped shape this document.

Acknowledgments

To Patrice Owens Parker, my sister, whose editorial skills were indispensable, and who told me family stories that brought this research to life. To Michaele Byrd, whose incredible talent and skill prepared this manuscript for publication.

To my sons, Christian and David Parker, who respected the time I needed to work on this effort. And finally, to my parents, Helen Viola West Owens and Dr. Hugo Armstrong Owens Sr., who inspired me with examples of resilience and resistance, taught me to be proud of my family history, to make faith foremost, to care about others and, if given the opportunity, to speak on their behalf.

Thank you.

Introduction

AFRICAN AMERICANS HAVE EXPERIENCED traumatic loss of lives, language, family, and culture as a result of the chattel slavery experience in North America. The historical, economic and political events that took place during this time and after emancipation in 1863 continue to contribute to the current social ills of high rates of incarceration, depression, domestic violence, unemployment, drug abuse, and homicide.

The effects of generational trauma have been identified and studied in the Jewish, Armenian, and Native American communities. Literature on the Jewish Holocaust, Armenian Genocide, Native American massacre at Wounded Knee, and the African American Slave Trade describes the intergenerational transmission of trauma, grief, and loss. Health care professionals, social scientists, historians, and theologians have identified economic, social, religious, cultural, and educational patterns of behavior that are processes perpetuated from generation to generation. By using the genogram, we begin to understand the inherited positive and negative patterns and their effects on the lives of the individuals, families, and communities.

The goal of this work was to develop six two-hour classes using the genogram as a tool to identify both trauma and triumphs to: 1) facilitate forgiveness, reconciliation, and healing of the wounded history; 2) recognize and honor a positive heritage; and 3) celebrate hope for future generations. The target group for this project was twelve African American church members in the Richmond, Virginia area who were willing to study a minimum of three generations in their families. The methods and interventions are based on modern Western treatment for chronic and multigenerational grieving and emotional pain. I used African, African American, and Christian rituals of healing, forgiveness, and reconciliation.

Introduction

I researched the social, cultural, psychological, and historical context of the effects of chronic emotional pain and transgenerational trauma induced by chattel slavery. I looked at how the effects have been passed down through generations in the African American church community in Richmond, Virginia. I reviewed the psychological issues around chronic trauma and historical pain and how it manifests itself from generation to generation. By researching family systems theory and the use of the genogram, I identified how chronic trauma and historical pain in families are transmitted. Using a theology of healing and redemption and the doctrine of *Imago Dei*, I explored the theological works of Matthew V. Johnson, Flora Keshgegian, Shelly Rambo, and Dominic Robinson.

PART I

Roots Matter: Healing History, Honoring Heritage, Renewing Hope

ORIGIN OF THE IDEA

I WAS FIRST INTRODUCED to the concept of generational healing when I attended a training for healing prayer ministers at Christian Healing Ministries (CHM) in Jacksonville, FL. Founded by Dr. Francis and Judith MacNutt, CHM is dedicated to praying for those in need of healing in the physical, emotional, and spiritual areas of their lives, and teaching others about this often overlooked aspect of Christ's ministry. I was familiar with the concept of generational curses and blessings in my own family religious tradition, African American Baptist; however, the systematic study of generational family relationships and patterns and a special healing service to pray for healing of those relationships and patterns were new to me. I was instructed in the use of the genogram to identify recurring circumstances and repetitive behavior and significant events in my family. I was given an extensive list describing family connections and incidents to help me recognize who and what in my family needed healing prayer. And, in the Episcopal tradition, a generational healing Eucharist was held to pray for the healing of those identified places of brokenness.

When I read Maurice Apprey's article, "The African-American Experience: Forced Immigration and Transgenerational Trauma"[1] a few years

---

1. Apprey, "The African-American Experience," 70–75.

Part I

later, I recognized the importance and relevance of this subject in the African American community. In his article, Apprey refers to the story of one family portrayed in the novel *Thereafter Johnnie* by Carolivia Herron.[2] Herron's novel is a biographical account of herself as a product of incest and of the six generations preceding her that began in rape. Having counseled and prayed with women who had sexual abuse and incest in their family history and had been victims themselves, I knew I wanted to pursue healing transgenerational trauma. Africans and African Americans experienced the brutality, inhumanity, savagery, and cruelty of chattel slavery for 246 years. Sexual abuse was only one of many traumas that occurred in the eight generations who lived and died during that time. The consequences of traumas are reflected in the emotional, physical, economic lives, and health of today's African American community.[3]

Healing is the alleviation of or relief from pain and brokenness wherein a person experiences therapeutic, medicinal, and/or spiritual health-giving restoration due to curative treatment and repair.[4] A significant part of healing is knowing personal, family, and cultural history. It identifies the strengths and weaknesses in the family and culture. It creates a solid sense of self, a "density of being," a groundedness in knowing one's self and all that it encompasses. It fosters empathy, forgiveness, tolerance, and acceptance of others. Understanding transgenerational trauma and how it affects the lives of the living and future generations lightens the previously unknown emotional, physical, and spiritual burdens of the past. Learning and practicing the spiritual discipline of generational healing prayer and its benefits creates a greater awareness of self in relation to family, community, culture, and God.

LIMITATION AND KEY ASSUMPTIONS

As a candidate in the Doctor of Ministry program at San Francisco Theological Seminary, I chose for my dissertation topic "Using the Genogram as a Tool for Healing of Transgenerational Trauma in the African American Church Community in Virginia" because I wanted to: a) underscore the importance of personal, family, and cultural history, and the profound

---

2. Herron, *Thereafter Johnnie*.
3. Institute for Research on Poverty, "Who is Poor?," http://www.irp.wisc.edu/faqs/faq3.htm.
4. See author's definition in glossary.

importance in recognizing its impact on lives; b) focus attention on the lasting effects of unresolved transgenerational trauma in individuals and families; and c) develop a generational healing service that incorporates African and African American culture. I wanted to give individuals and families another approach to breaking generations of traumatized learned behavior and attitudes so they can bring about a restored, repaired, and renewed identity that gives them the ability to provide a more stable, less stressful way of life for themselves and future generations.

I limited the scope of my study to chattel slavery in Virginia from 1619 to 1865 because: 1) my advisor strongly suggested that my initial topic was too broad and would eventually become unmanageable, and 2) I am familiar with the two regions of the state that are pertinent to the more focused topic. My ancestors were from plantations in the Chesapeake area of Virginia where chattel slavery began in North America in 1619, and I currently live in Richmond, Virginia. The historical resources in both locations were a major factor in developing the curriculum. Of all the states in the Confederacy, Virginia was, by far, the leading exporter of slaves to other southern states by the antebellum era. "In terms of capitalization, the slave trade centered in Richmond was the largest single variable in the national economy. In 1858, Templeton and Goodwin's auction business in Richmond generated nearly $3 million in gross sales in 2011 dollars. Some months saw as many as 10,000 slaves bought, sold or hired out in Richmond alone."[5]

The genogram is a pictorial display of physical, psychological, spiritual, behavioral hereditary patterns visualized and identified through a systematic method of recording family history and relationships.[6] Created by Maury Bowen, who developed the family systems theory, and Monica McGoldrick, who expanded his concept, the genogram helps distinguish family relationships and arrangements of significant events in families.[7] This tool will assist the family member in recognizing the traumatic situations and unhealthy relationships that need healing prayer and also recognize the strengths, talents, and achievements that need to be celebrated in the family.

---

5. Trammell, *Richmond Slave Trade*, 28.
6. See author's definition in glossary.
7. Bowen Center, "Theory."

Part I

ETHICAL METHODOLOGY

The project segment of the Doctor of Ministry (DMin) requirements was a six-week, two-hour class. The class was an exploratory exercise in developing a method to attend to the transgenerational trauma of the transatlantic and domestic slave trade within the context of the African American church community in Virginia. Chattel slavery was designed, developed and implemented in Virginia. The traumatic impact of chattel slavery on the enslaved Africans and African Americans, and its effect on subsequent generations was the focus of this class. Studies of the Jewish Holocaust, Native American massacres, the Armenian Genocide, and the African American slave trade describe the intergenerational transmission of trauma, grief, and loss. Health care professionals, social scientists, historians, and theologians have identified economic, social, religious, cultural, and educational patterns of behavior that are processes perpetuated from generation to generation.[8]

The class objectives were to: a) understand the lasting effects of trauma; b) recognize the importance of family history and how it influences the present; c) appreciate the resiliency of the human spirit and the healing power of faith and prayer; and d) design a spiritual discipline to facilitate healing of transgenerational trauma in the African American church community.

The desired class size was ten to twelve participants, small enough to create safety and intimacy, yet large enough to be a viable group if there were absences. Twenty were invited; twelve were actual participants. Because this was a pilot class using sensitive and evocative material that had not been presented in this particular context, the decision was made to have participants who knew the DMin candidate. This would encourage a sense of familiarity, trust, and safety. All of the students were colleagues in ministry or had professional relationships with each other. There were two men and ten women. The age range was thirty to eighty years. Six were ordained clergy (none were pastors), and six were lay people. Two were high school graduates with professional training in their businesses; one held a PhD, and the remaining held one or more Master's degrees. Professions represented were chaplaincy, information technology, hospital administration, nonprofit executive and program management, educational

---

8. For further reading see Cloud and Townsend, *Secrets of Your Family Tree*; Hintz, *Healing Your Family History*; Newberg et. al., *Why God Won't Go Away*; Rothschild, *Body Remembers*; Scaer, *The Body Bears the Burden*.

consulting, physical therapy, massage therapy, and carpentry. There were three Presbyterians and nine Baptists.

Chapter 1
Family Systems, Genogram, and Biblical Examples

INITIALLY, THE EUROPEANS HAD no master plan for slavery or sources of labor to satisfy the demand for sugar. The first African slaves arrived from Europe—not Africa—in the early 1500s. It was not until the mid-1520s that the first slave ship sailed directly from Africa to northern Brazil. Until that time, Amerindians were the source of labor on the sugar plantations. Brazil and the Caribbean became the center of the Atlantic Slave Trade System using 90 percent of all enslaved Africans for the production of sugar. The countries that were the sources of enslaved people were: Senegambia, 6 percent; Sierra Leone, 3.1 percent; the Windward Coast, 2.7 percent; Gold Coast, 9.7 percent; Bight of Benin, 16 percent; Bight of Biafra, 12.7 percent; West Central Africa (Congo), 45 percent; St. Helena southeast Africa, and the Indian Ocean Islands (Mozambique), 4.3 percent.[1]

The United States imported less than 4 percent (an estimated 388,747) of the total number of Africans transported. However, in 1860, the United States had 3,954,000 enslaved people, the largest number of people of African descent ever assembled in the New World. Seventy-five percent of these enslaved people worked as agricultural laborers growing cotton, sugar, rice, tobacco, and hemp. The majority of these worked in cotton. About 15 percent of southern slaves were classified as domestic servants, and approximately 10 percent worked in commerce, trades, and industry—principally in towns and cities. The transatlantic trade reached its peak in the late 1700s. Under the influence of the abolitionist reformers, the United

---

1. Eltis and Richardson, *Atlas of the Transatlantic Slave Trade*, xix, 15.

States and Britain outlawed slavery in 1808. However, some three million Africans, one-fourth of the total exported, were shipped to the Americas after 1807 despite the militant attempts of the British navy.[2]

The enormity of human suffering caused by this crime against humanity is indescribable. The human misery quotient generated by the forced movement of millions of people in slave ships during the Middle Passage cannot have been matched by any other human activity. On the slave ships, sexes were separated, kept naked, packed close together, and the men were chained for long periods. No less than 26 percent of those on board were classed as children, a ratio that no other pre-twentieth-century migration could come close to matching. The average duration of voyages from all regions of Africa was just over two months. Throughout the slave trade era, filthy conditions ensured endemic gastrointestinal diseases, and a range of epidemic pathogens that, together with periodic breakouts of violent resistance, meant that between 12 and 13 percent of those who embarked did not survive the voyage.[3] These statistics illustrate the atrocious magnitude, longevity, and diversity of trauma experienced by the Africans brought to the Americas and Caribbean. They describe the massive injury to the spirit, psyche, and memory of the African people. These facts and figures detail the suffering that continues to be carried in the bodies, minds, and ethos of their descendants.

Ron Eyerman, Professor of Sociology and Co-Director of the Center for Cultural Sociology at Yale University, writes in his article "The Past in the Present: Culture and the Transmission of Memory":

> Like memory, the notion of trauma, or deeply felt emotional response to some occurrence, has both individual and collective connotation. Alexander ('Introduction' op cit.) speaks of a cultural trauma when members of a collective feel they have been subjected to a horrendous event that leaves indelible marks upon their group consciousness, marking their memories forever, and changing their future identity in fundamental and irrevocable ways . . . As opposed to psychological or physical trauma which involves a wound and the experience of great emotional anguish by an individual, cultural trauma refers to a dramatic loss of identity and meaning, a tear in the social fabric, affecting a group of people who have achieved some degree of cohesion. In this sense,

---

2. Ibid., xx–xxi.
3. Ibid., xxv.

Part I

the trauma need not necessarily be felt by everyone in a group or have been directly experienced by any or all.[4]

Cultural trauma as defined by Neil Smelser is:

> A memory accepted and publicly given credence by a relevant membership group and evoking an event or situation which is (a) laden with negative affect, (b) represented as indelible, and (c) regarded as threatening a society's [or group's] existence or violating one or more of its fundamental cultural presuppositions.[5]

There are many recorded slave narratives that describe what they experienced and what they saw during the 352 years (1514–1866) of transatlantic slave trade.[6] One of the most comprehensive descriptions of what happened to those captured and sold is told by Ouobna Ottobah Cugoano, an African abolitionist who lived in the mid-eighteenth century in England. He tells the story of his experience of capture, in the slave castle and on the slave ship before he landed in Grenada and was bought by an Englishman.

> I was early snatched away from my native country, with about eighteen or twenty more boys and girls, as we were playing in a field. We lived but a few days' journey from the coast where we were kidnapped, and as we were decoyed and drove along, we were soon conducted to a factory, and from thence, in the fashionable way of traffic, consigned to Grenada ... (T)he horrors I soon saw and felt, cannot be well described; I saw many of my miserable countrymen chained two and two, some handcuffed, and some with their hands tied behind. We were conducted along by a guard, and when we arrived at the castle, I asked my guard what I was brought there for, he told me to learn the ways of the browfow, that is, the white-faced people. I saw him take a gun, a piece of cloth, and some lead for me, and then he told me that he must now leave me there, and went off. This made me cry bitterly, but I was soon conducted to a prison, for three days, where I heard the groans and cries of many, and saw some of my fellow-captives. But when a vessel arrived to conduct us away to the ship, it was a most horrible scene; there was nothing to be heard but the rattling of chains, smacking of whips, and the groans and cries of our fellow-men.

---

4. Eyerman, "The Past in the Present," 159–69.
5. Ibid., 162.
6. Eltis and Halbert, "Transatlantic Slave Trade Data Base."

Family Systems, Genogram, and Biblical Examples

Some would not stir from the ground, when they were lashed and beat in the most horrible manner.[7]

The Africans' history and traditions were disrupted by the transatlantic slave trade and slavery. Language, climate, world view, family, community, religion, and ethics had to be reinvented in a way that fostered their survival. They were forced to create a new history and new traditions in the confines of the harsh strange culture.

The people of Ghana West Africa were 9.7 percent of Africans who were transported to the Americas and the Caribbean. The Akan people are an ethnic group found predominantly in the Gold Coast which today is Ghana and the Ivory Coast.[8] The Asante are one of the sub-groups of the Akan. The Asante created Adinkra symbols that represent a proverb or a wise saying. The Sankofa, one of the Adinkra symbols, is the image of a bird whose body is heading in one direction and whose head is turned in the opposite direction. The image is interpreted to mean, "We cannot go forward without first looking back to our past to understand how we have gotten to where we are."[9]

Carl Jung believed that the strongest psychic effect on children is the life their parents have not lived. "Children . . . re-enact under unconscious compulsion the unlived lives of their parents . . . the lives the parents didn't know, didn't dare or denied to exist. Without being conscious of it, without being able to articulate just what is going on, children pick up their parents' failure to live authentically, and take on this burden."[10] Cultural legacies are powerful forces that have deep roots and long lives. Customs and traditions persist, generation after generation virtually intact, even as the economic and social and demographic conditions that gave rise to them have vanished. Habits and historical conventions play such a role in directing attitudes and behavior that we cannot make sense of the world without them.

Whether we are an only child, or come from a family with many brothers and sisters, or adopted, fostered, or grew up in a group home, we have all been shaped by our family group story. We carry within us a mixed bag of good and bad memories, and they continue to shape our daily responses to life. There will be some form of expression of the repeated pattern of

---

7. Cugoano, *Narrative of the Enslavement*, 121–24.
8. Eltis and Richardson, *Atlas of the Transatlantic Slave Trade*, 15.
9. Fosu, *Handbook on Kente Designs*, 31.
10. Jungian Center for the Spiritual Sciences, "Jung on the Problem Child," http://jungiancenter.org/jung-on-the-problem-child/.

Part I

our family group story which will influence us from time to time. Values like independence or dependence, working hard or just enough to get by, doing the right thing or seeing how much you can get away with, are sown into us and later reaped in the way we live our lives as adults. We carry the tensions, behaviors, values, and attitudes with us as we move through life, and sometimes we unconsciously create situations that are very similar Ron Eyerman writes:

> All nations and groups have founding myths, stories which tell who we are through recounting where we came from. Such narratives form "master frames" and are passed on through traditions, in rituals and ceremonies, public performances which re-connect a group, and where membership is confirmed. Within this process, "we" are re-membered and "they" are excluded. Founding narratives are about creating, constituting a collective subject as much as they are about creating an "imagined" community. Slavery is a cultural marker, a primal scene and a site of memory in the formation of African American identity . . . Slavery is a site of memory for African-Americans requiring constant reflection and reinterpretation. It is an historic event present in every African American's consciousness. Different generations have different perspectives on the past because of both emotional and temporal distance, altered circumstances and needs but all generations of African Americans need to interpret and come to terms with their collective traumatic past and their relationship to that past. Cultural trauma is evident in the group, public memory of slavery, and its aftermath.[11]

Michele Norris, reporter on National Public Radio program *All Things Considered* took note of the fact that President Obama's historic election prompted the conversation about race in America. Her initial focus for writing her book, *The Grace of Silence*, was to capture what was being said in these conversations. She found, as she worked with groups, that something was always left unsaid. She writes, "Filters would automatically engage, preventing us from saying things that might cause embarrassment or get us into trouble, or even worse, reveal us for who we really are. We weren't so much talking about race as talking around it. What I did not know until I began this project is that I was also shaped by the weight of my parent's silence."[12]

---

11. Eyerman, "The Past in the Present," 164–67.
12. Norris, *The Grace of Silence*, 22.

Family Systems, Genogram, and Biblical Examples

Norris tells the story about her uncle who told her after her father died that her father had been shot by white police right after he came home from World War II. Because of the incident, her father and his five brothers had to leave Birmingham only days after his coming home. Michele's father never told his wife. He never said anything to anyone. After hearing the story from her uncle, Norris began to see her father from a new perspective and with new questions. "Was his walk with the lilt in his step from the gunshot wound or was it just the characteristic gait a lot of black men have? Was he really a peacemaker always wanting to dispel conflict or was his behavior as peacemaker an act of desperation, satisfying a deep seated need to avoid the mind's darker places? Benevolence, for some, can be a survival tactic."[13] These questions and others led Norris to research her family story and discover the details of that event, and how it had affected her and her extended family.

Originally developed in the field of psychology with victims of abuse and war, the interest in trauma has now expanded into the fields of history, literature, biblical studies, theology, sociology, and neuroscience.[14] Trauma affects the mind, the spirit, and the body, consciously and unconsciously. As can be seen in the stories of Ouobna Ottobah Cugoano and Michelle Norris, and with the studies and research that have been done in the past thirty-five years, we know now that such horror and abuse that were afflicted on the captured Africans have been passed down through the generations, and there is much that the present generations carry in their bodies and in their unconscious. The constant retraumatization that occurs daily is an incredible psychic burden that most people do not know they are carrying.[15]

It was Sigmund Freud who drew attention to what he called "the repetition compulsion," the all-too-human tendency to repeat the past. He connected it to traumatic experience and pointed out that through their actions, people unconsciously repeat the past.[16] We, as a society, do not for the most part recognize how much of the past we are carrying, and how deeply it is embedded in our morals, values, lifestyle, and worldview. Statements like "You act just like your grandfather" or "She is an old soul" or "He is a chip off the old block" are popular ways in which we do see the past in the present; but most of us truly do not realize that we are looking at behaviors

---

13. Ibid., 22.
14. Rambo, *Spirit and Trauma*, 3.
15. For further reading see Rothschild, *Body Remembers*, 37–64.
16. Herman, *Trauma and Recovery*, 41–42.

which are accumulations from generations, and that some of those behaviors are positive and some are negative. Fortunately, there are tools and theories that can help us unpack the stories and bring to consciousness and awareness what we are doing to ourselves and each other which enable us to make significant positive and healthy changes to ourselves, our descendants, and the world around us.

FAMILY SYSTEMS THEORY

Murray Bowen, M.D., 1913–1990, was a pioneer in family therapy and the developer of a systems theory of the family. Bowen perceived families as arrangements of interconnected and interdependent individuals, none of whom could be understood in isolation from the way the relationships of all the persons functioned as a whole. Human beings could not be understood in isolation from one another, but rather as a part of a larger group emotional unit. Within the boundaries of the group, patterns develop as certain member's behavior is caused by and causes other member's behaviors in predictable ways. Maintaining the same pattern of relationships could lead to either healthy or unhealthy behavior.[17]

Bowen found that when anyone in the family emotional system began to make more individual responsible choices, he or she would be attacked by others. First there would be accusations of being selfish, then of denying anything happened to cause a need to change, and then in anger, threatens to leave or harm oneself. Often the person attempting to make a healthy change would be intimidated into submission. It might take several attempts before the person would be able to follow through with the new decision and then would only be able to act with support. If the change is successful, then another family member might follow suit and initiate another systemic change.[18]

There are eight interlocking concepts in Bowen's theory: triangles, nuclear family emotional system, family projection process, societal emotional process, emotional cutoff, sibling position, differentiation of self, and multigenerational transmission process. I will focus on two of Bowen's concepts—differentiation of self and the multigenerational transmission process—because these concepts highlight the influence family members

---

17. Bowen Center, "Theory."
18. Sears, "Healing Family," 3.

have on each other, and how they consciously and unconsciously reinforce patterns of behavior and values from one generation to the next.

DIFFERENTIATION OF SELF

Differentiation of self is the ability to single out one's personhood from the group by drawing distinctions between self and others because there is an innate desire to become an authentic individual. The basic building blocks of a "self" are inborn, but an individual's family relationships during childhood and adolescence primarily determine how much "self" he or she develops. Once established, the level of "self" rarely changes unless a person makes a structured and long-term effort to change it. Bowen identifies four main types of differentiation: 1) Low—People of low differentiation have very little sense of self outside the relationship system. They are people pleasers who spend all their energy seeking approval and acceptance. 2) Moderate—People who are guided by accepted tradition and law. Lacking a solid "self" conviction about the world, they will often quote rules and scientific fact to make their point. 3) Good—Those who can hold their own under peer pressure, who can participate in emotional relationships with confidence and have the ability to remove themselves if the need arises. 4) High—Bowen considers people with high differentiation as more hypothetical than real. It is more what he or she is not. They are not the "rugged individualist" which he describes as a "pretend" posture of those who are fighting against the "system." People of high differentiation are always aware of others and the relationships around them. However, they recognize their dependence on others. Confident in their thinking, they can either support another's view without being a disciple or reject another's view without polarizing the differences.[19]

MULTIGENERATIONAL TRANSMISSION PROCESS

Bowen defines the multigenerational transmission process as "the concept that describes how small differences in the levels of differentiation between parents and their offspring lead to marked differences over many generations among the members of a multigenerational family. The information creating these differences is transmitted across generations through

19. Bowen Center, "Differentiation of Self."

Part I

relationships. The transmission occurs on several interconnected levels ranging from the conscious teaching and learning of information to the automatic and unconscious programming of emotional reactions and behaviors. Relationally and genetically transmitted information interact to shape an individual's "self." The combination of parents actively shaping the development of their offspring, of offspring innately responding to their parents' moods, attitudes, and actions, and of the long dependency period of human offspring results in people developing levels of differentiation of self, similar to their parents' levels. However, the relationship patterns of nuclear family emotional systems often result in at least one member of a sibling group developing a little more "self" and another member developing a little less "self" than the parents."[20] The following example illustrates how family patterns of behavior can be passed on unconsciously.

> Jenna's life began with a secret: Her father, known as a player around his Detroit neighborhood, hid Jenna's existence from his own parents and siblings until he fell ill in 1998. Six years later, Jenna, then thirty and living in Oakland, discovered that yet another man was keeping her a secret. She was eight months pregnant when Allen, the clean-cut investment banker she had been dating for a year, came home one day and confessed, "I'm married and I have two children." For years, Allen revealed, he had maintained two apartments—one with his wife of ten years and their 5- and 8-year-old daughters, and another for his sexual forays. When he first told me the truth said Jenna, "I went numb." Perhaps even more disturbing was Jenna's realization that she was repeating an old pattern: Allen had entangled her in a web of lies and denial, just as her father once had. "I always seem to get myself in situations where I am the hidden one, the secret," says Jenna, who has a history of dating men already involved with other women. She was also a survivor of sexual abuse: Between ages 7 and 12, she was molested by a married man who was an acquaintance of her mother. During college, after a particularly bad breakup, Jenna entered therapy and began to connect the dots. "I finally saw what I was doing," she says. "I chose men who were not available to me, men who couldn't commit, were dishonest, and had secret lives. I never felt like I was chosen by my father, and I kept repeating that pattern in my relationships."[21]

20. Bowen Center, "Multigenerational Transmission Process."
21. Roberts, "Ghosts of Relationships," 88.

According to Bowen, people predictably select mates with levels of differentiation of self that match their own. Therefore, if one sibling's level of "self" is higher and another sibling's level of "self" is lower than the parents, one sibling's marriage is more independent in family relationships, and the other sibling's marriage is more dependent in family relationships than the parents' marriage. If each sibling then has a child who is more differentiated or independent and a child who is less differentiated or dependent than himself or herself, one generational line becomes progressively more differentiated (the most differentiated child of the most differentiated sibling) and one line becomes progressively less differentiated (the least differentiated child of the least differentiated sibling). As these processes repeat over multiple generations, the differences between family lines grow increasingly marked.[22]

Fr. Robert Sears, S.J., Ph.D., adjunct professor at Loyola University's Institute of Pastoral Studies writes in his article, "Healing and Family Spiritual/Emotional Systems,"

> The less differentiated the family the more inherited patterns will be handed down unreflectively from one generation to the next. People tend to marry others who have a similar sense of self (low, moderate or high). A person with too high a sense of self is too threatening and one with too low is uninteresting. When both partners have weak "solid selves," their lack of awareness causes them to withdraw, to cling (become dominated), or to fight in cyclical fashion instead of working out their differences. What remains unconscious, especially when the family is under pressure, "triangles" others into the emotional interaction. An unhappy wife might unburden her anger at her husband on her daughter or son, or a daughter might be drawn to fulfill the emotional needs of her father which are unmet by his wife. The "triangle" child has little emotional space for his or her own self-discovery, and becomes absorbed into the implied viewpoint of the system ("men cannot be trusted," or "mothers are to be supported," etc.). He or she then marries someone who corresponds to this family pattern, and they in turn hand it on to their children . . . (Bowen estimates that the variation among family members would be about 10 percent more or less differentiated, or there may be a gradual degeneration which could result in severe loss of "solid self" or psychosis which he estimated would take seven generations or more). To unravel a multigenerational pattern, a diagram of one's family can help

---

22. Bowen Center "Differentiation of Self."

to identify past traumas (suicides, divorces, mental breakdowns, etc.) and defense patterns (denial, absorption/dominance, conflict/closeness) that are repeated and to see where the emotional closeness or antagonism has been. The healing process aims then, at increasing the member's ability to become aware of the patterns they are living in order to make more individually responsible decisions. Bowen provides an overall framework for seeing the family emotional system around certain variables: sense of self, in continuing relationship and multigenerational patterning.[23]

THE GENOGRAM

The genogram is a pictorial display in which physical, psychological, spiritual, and behavioral hereditary patterns are visualized and identified through a systematic method of recording family history and relationships. Genograms were first developed by Murray Bowen in the 1970s, and popularized in clinical settings by Monica McGoldrick and Randy Gerson through the publication of the first edition *Genograms: Assessment and Intervention* in 1985. In an attempt to reflect the increasingly complex relationships in families, a second edition was published in 1999 and a third in 2008.

Studying patterns of behavior and how they relate to those of a multigenerational family, reveals new and more effective options for solving problems and for changing responses to the automatic role a family member is expected to play. They contain the basic data found in family trees such as the name, gender, date of birth, and date of death of each individual. However, genograms are designed to include additional data such as education, occupation, major life events, chronic illnesses, social behaviors, nature of family relationships, emotional relationships, spiritual relationships, and social relationships. Some genograms also include information on disorders running in the family such as alcoholism, depression, diseases, alliances, and living situations. Genograms can vary significantly since there is no limitation as to what type of data can be recorded. They are now used by various groups of people in a variety of fields such as medicine, psychology, social work, genealogy, genetic research, and education.[24] Using the genogram, the physician can prescribe a treatment, the psychologist or therapist

---

23. Sears "Healing Family," 15.
24. For further reading see McGoldrick, *Genograms*.

can provide insight and coping strategies, and people of faith can prescribe prayer for generational healing.

SCRIPTURE

There is evidence in scripture that illustrates a multigenerational transmission process in the references to the transmission of a) positive traits referred to as blessings—favorable characteristics and circumstances as results of good choices, inherited skills, gifts, talents, and grace, and b) negative traits referred to as curses—adverse attributes and situations that occurred because of poor choices, trauma, untimely deaths, disease, and lack of resources.

Examples of the belief in the transmission of blessing and curses are found in Exodus 20:5-6, "You shall not bow down to them (idols) or worship them; for I, the LORD your God, am a jealous God, punishing children for the iniquity of parents, to the third and the fourth generation of those who reject me, but showing love to a thousand generations of those who love me and keep my commandments," and in Psalm 103:17, "But the steadfast love of the LORD is from everlasting to everlasting on those who fear him, and his righteousness to children's children, to those who keep his covenant and remember to do his commandments.."[25]

Examples of generational blessings can be found in Genesis 48:15-16, in which Israel (Jacob) blesses Joseph's sons, Ephraim and Manasseh. He blessed Joseph, and said, "The God before whom my ancestors Abraham and Isaac walked, the God who has been my shepherd all my life to this day, the angel who has redeemed me from all harm, bless the boys; and in them let my name be perpetuated, and the names of my ancestors Abraham and Isaac; and let them grow into a multitude on the earth."

Isaiah prophesies to the exiles a blessing in Isaiah 44:1-5, "But now hear, O Jacob my servant, Israel whom I have chosen! Thus says the LORD who made you, who formed you in the womb and will help you: Do not fear, O Jacob my servant, Jeshurun whom I have chosen. For I will pour water on the thirsty land, and streams on the dry ground; I will pour my spirit upon your descendants, and my blessing on your offspring. They shall spring up like a green tamarisk, like willows by flowing streams. This one will say, 'I am the LORD's,' another will be called by the name of Jacob, yet another will write on the hand, 'The LORD's,' and adopt the name of Israel."

25. All biblical references are from the New Revised Standard Version 1989.

Part I

In 2 Timothy 1:3–5, Paul recognized Timothy's gift of faith passed on from grandmother to mother to son. "I am grateful to God—whom I worship with a clear conscience, as my ancestors did—when I remember you constantly in my prayers night and day. Recalling your tears, I long to see you so that I may be filled with joy. I am reminded of your sincere faith, a faith that lived first in your grandmother, Lois, and your mother, Eunice, and now, I am sure, lives in you."

Examples of the transmission of generational patterns can be interpreted in the family and descendants of Abram and Sarai, and even though conditions of the time and culture are great influences on behavior, there are some basic family relationships that are common, if not universal and timeless.

The First Generation—Abram and Sarai (Genesis 16:1–16; 17:15–22; 21:1–21)

In this family narrative, Sarai, Abram's wife, cannot conceive. She takes matters in her own hands and has Abram sleep with Hagar, her maidservant. Hagar becomes pregnant and has a son, Ishmael. Sarai and Hagar have a hostile relationship after Ishmael is born, and Hagar runs away. God sends her back with a promise of Ishmael becoming the father of many descendants. Sarai becomes pregnant by Abram and has a son Isaac. Sarai favors Isaac because he is her biological child. Abram wanted Ishmael to be an equal part of the family, but Sarai would not allow it. Isaac's birth was celebrated but not Ishmael's. The favoritism of the younger child triggers sibling rivalry. Sarai, believing that Isaac's blessing and inheritance is threatened, forces Hagar and Ishmael out of the family home. Abram, a father who did not stand by Ishmael in times of dispute, diminishes Ishmael's sense of self-worth and poisons his future relationships with him and Ishmael's relationship with Isaac.

The Second Generation—Isaac and Rebekah (Genesis 24; 25:19–34; 27:41–45; 33:1, 12–20)

Rebekah, Isaac's wife, has difficulty conceiving, but eventually gives birth to twin boys. Isaac favors Esau, the older twin, and Rebekah favors Jacob, the younger twin. Sibling rivalry surfaces again between Jacob and Esau, and they become pawns in the parental struggle over the inheritance, the same struggle between Ishmael and Isaac in the previous generation. At his mother's prompting, Jacob tricks Esau and his father into bestowing on him the blessing of the first born that should have been Esau's. Isaac's history of being the mother's favorite and receiving the inheritance is repeated with Jacob. Jacob, the younger child, is forced to leave home. The reason is different: Jacob stole Esau's inheritance rather than being denied an inheritance as Ishmael had, but the struggle was again over the inheritance.

The Third Generation—Jacob and Rachel (Genesis 29:16–28; 29:31—30:25; 35:16–20; 37:17b–28)

In the third generation, trickery is repeated. Jacob runs away to live with his uncle Laban. Jacob tricks Laban into an agreement that results in Jacob getting the better flocks of sheep and goats. Jacob is then tricked by Laban into marrying Leah, his older daughter, and then tricks him again into working seven more years in order to marry Rachel, the younger daughter, whom Jacob really loved. There is tension between Rachel and Leah as there was with Sarai and Hagar in the competition of childbirth, which included their maidservants. Jacob favors Rachel and her children, Joseph and Benjamin. Sibling rivalry occurs among the other brothers. Joseph is sold into slavery, and once again, a child is forced to leave home.

What do these family group stories say about the men and fathers in these families and how they treat their sons? What about their choice of wives? What about the relationships the men have with the other women in the stories? What do these stories say about the mother/son relationships and their power and control over their husbands and sons?

Sears raises this question, "What is the interdependence between generations, and how are we freed from the negative patterns for new life in Christ?" Looking first at the Old Testament, Sears identifies three key attributes in the family relationships of the Israelites: 1) their corporate personality, 2) the Old Testament formula: "Unto the fourth generation," and 3) the recognition of individual responsibility. Referencing H. Wheeler Robinson, an Old Testament British scholar who developed the concept of corporate personality,[26] Sears describes four characteristics of corporate personality: a) the corporate personality extends beyond the present to the past and future. The Patriarchs Abraham, Isaac, and Jacob are unifying

---

26. For further reading see Robinson, *Corporate Personality*.

Part I

presences in the nation that carries their name, honor, and life. As Jacob ages he says, "I am to be gathered unto my kindred" (Gen 49:29). Ancestors and contemporaries are seen as one family.[27]

Eyerman states, "Slavery is a cultural marker, a primal scene and a site of memory in the formation of African American identity. Succeeding generations of African American intellectuals have formed their own sense of identity and mission as they have reflected upon and reinterpreted its meaning. In the process, they articulated and reconstituted the collective narrative."[28] Examples of historical figures that provide a unifying presence in the African American corporate identity are Gabriel Prosser, Nat Turner, Harriet Tubman, Ida B. Wells, and Fredrick Douglass.[29] b) The unity of individual and community is so realistically conceived that it can be concentrated in a single representative figure. There is more than a moral bond. It is as real as blood ties, an unconscious instinctive bonding. The David and Goliath challenge is the challenge of the Philistines and Israel (1 Sam 17:8). A classic example in the African American community is the Joe Louis vs Max Schmeling heavyweight boxing match.[30] c) There is a fluid passing from individual to collective and vice versa as though each was seen in the other. The "suffering servant" of second Isaiah is both singular and plural. Current examples of this are the murder of Treyvon Martin,[31] and the silent prayer—"Please don't let them be black"—that African Americans say when there are crimes, especially sensational crimes, reported on the evening news. d) The leader is representative of the group as intercessor as well as an individual, such as Moses and the prophets. "Race men [and women]," a term from the beginning of the twentieth century, described black men [and women] of stature and integrity who represented the best that African Americans had to offer in the face of Jim Crow segregation. They represented an unspoken measure of commitment to uplifting the race. Race men [and women] inspire pride; their work, their actions, and their speech represent excellence instead of evoking shame and embarrassment. Benjamin Mays, Mordecai Johnson, Carter G. Woodson, Maggie

---

27. Sears, "Healing Family," 15.

28. Eyerman, "The Past in the Present, 160–61.

29. For further reading see Franklin and Higginbotham, *From Slavery to Freedom*.

30. For further reading see the official website of Joe Louis: http://www.cmgww.com/sports/louis/bio.htm.

31. "Florida Teen Shooting," http://www.cnn.com/2012/05/18/justice/florida-teen-shooting-details/index.html.

Walker, Mary McLeod Bethune, and Zora Neale Hurston were leaders representative of the group.[32]

The second attribute of family relationship in the Old Testament is the formula "Unto four generations" referred to in the scripture, "I, the LORD your God, am a jealous God visiting the iniquity of the fathers upon the children to the third and fourth generation but showing steadfast love to thousands of those who love me and keep my commandments" (Exod 20:5–6; 34:6–8; Num 14:18; Deut 5:1–10) This notion is especially important for understanding the transference of generational patterns. In the pre-exilic texts, the family head was seen in his offspring, not only for blessing as with Abraham and his offspring (Gen 12:1–3; 22:15–18), but also for punishment as when David took a census of the people and all Israel was punished (2 Sam 24:10–17). Even when personal responsibility is affirmed, the theme of the "sins of the father" is still emphasized. However, it is important to note that the offspring are said to repeat the sins of their father. Both have chosen. What the fathers began is continued in the sons' choices. In the minds of the priestly redactors, there exists a veritable identity between different generations: "Those of you who survive in the lands of their enemies will waste away for their own and their father's guilt" (Lev 26:39). Hence, they are to confess also their fathers' sins (Lev 26:40). Ezekiel, who stresses individual responsibility, still has Yahweh say: "They [the children of Israel] and their fathers have revolted against me to this very day" (Ezek 2:3). And Jeremiah can say: "Yahweh repays the father's guilt, even into the lap of their sons who follow" (Jer 32:18). We see here the basis for the Old Testament view of offspring continuing Adam's sin, which Paul develops in Rom 5:12–21.[33]

The frequency of genealogies shows the importance put on continuity of tradition. In Deuteronomy, the people are to "Go, and occupy the land I swore to your fathers, Abraham, Isaac, and Jacob, I would give to them and to their descendants" (Deut 1:8; 6:10; 9:5, 27; 34:4). God sees the fathers and their descendants as though in one glance. His love "for your fathers" led him to choose "you, their descendants . . ." (Deut 10:15). He extends his blessing to all. The command of the Decalogue to "honor your father and your mother so that you may have a long life in the land that Yahweh, your God, has given you" (Exod 20:21) reflects this promise of blessing. It is the first commandment with a promise connected to it rather than a

32. For further reading see Franklin and Higginbotham, *From Slavery to Freedom*.
33. Sears, "Healing Family," 16.

Part I

theological explanation, as Eph. 6:2 observes. The word "honor" indicates a wide, positive interpretation: to "obey" but also "prize highly" (Prov 4:8), "show respect," "glorify and exalt." It also has nuances of caring for and showing affection (Ps 91:15).[34]

The third attribute of family relationships in the Old Testament is recognizing individual responsibility. The exile released for Israel a new sense of individual responsibility. Ezekiel has Yahweh repeal the saying about the fathers eating sour grapes and setting the children's teeth on edge (Ezek 18). Each is rewarded or punished according to his or her own choices. Ezekiel 14:12–23 corrects the view that Yahweh is "unjust" for punishing the land even though there are just to be found there. The just will save only themselves and the land will be punished, but a remnant of righteousness will be left to reveal Yahweh's righteousness. Even Deut 7:10 and 24:16 affirm individual responsibility despite previously citing the formula about the guilt of the fathers. What is affirmed is the freedom to repent. Only the one who sins will be punished. It was not to be understood as only one choice—the father's—but the sons and offspring also have sinned by following his example.[35]

Looking at the New Testament, Sears notes Jesus breaks with tradition. He teaches to leave mother, father, sister etc. for the sake of the Kingdom (Mark 10:28–30). Jesus came not to bring peace but the sword . . . to set a man against his father, daughter against her mother (Matt 10:34–46, Luke 12:51–53). Both Matthew and Luke portray Jesus' virginal conception as a "new beginning" through the creative power of the Spirit, and Jesus' individuated relationship to the Father ultimately leads to his separation from even close ties of relationships when he is abandoned on the cross. He is called to a total centering on God.[36] Jesus separates himself from his family and tells his followers they will have to do the same because it is about being individuated from his family and centering exclusively on God . . . the ultimate in relationships.

Jesus is linked to the history of the people but not the immediate family. It is as if he is taking the development of faith as the next step past Ezekiel and Jeremiah's take on individual responsibility. The genealogy that Matthew writes takes him back to Abraham; the genealogy that Luke writes takes him back to Adam. The temptations in the wilderness are tests to

34. Ibid., 17.
35. Ibid., 15.
36. Ibid., 18.

individuate from human relationships. Matthew sees Jesus as Moses, Priest, and King and the temptations are to feed people (Moses), do miracles (Priest), rule (King). In each case, Jesus counteracts with Old Testament tradition by quoting Deuteronomy. Luke sees him as Messiah. Jesus bears the weight of his tradition, but responds in a new way in total fidelity to his Father.[37]

Jesus is head of a new people. Jesus heads the community of the people of the Spirit. Jesus frees us from familial and national bonds to create a new people. The connection is not the law but something greater, the Holy Spirit. Connection by the Holy Spirit supersedes the power of the law, but in following the Holy Spirit, the law is automatically fulfilled. For Paul, Jesus is the new Adam (1 Cor 15:45). For Luke, Jesus is the Messiah (Acts 2:32–36). For John, Jesus is the Word who was with the Father in the beginning, and to all who believe in Him, He gave power to become "children of God" (the new community) (John 1:12). "Jesus' (and our) freeing from familial relationships is not to lead to isolation, but to creativity in bringing about a new community in the Spirit. As we individuate from our families through prayer for the ancestors, we influence the families to become part of a healed and renewed community. . . . The pattern is separation from natural ties, new centering in Jesus' Spirit, and renewal of spiritual community."[38]

Bowen psychologically and Sears biblically reveal examples of how we are influenced by our ancestors. We imitate and adopt their values, attitudes, beliefs, habits, and behaviors passed down the generations consciously or unconsciously. There may be modifications, permutations, and combinations of these behaviors, but the influence is still there, and some are positive and others negative. The negative attitudes, values, behaviors, and beliefs block positive growth and development for ourselves and our descendants. If they are recognized, which is the first step towards healing, then there is an opportunity for reconciliation and freedom to develop healthy relationships in families and their descendants.

---

37. Ibid., 19.
38. Ibid.

Chapter 2
Generational Trauma in Jewish, Armenian, and Native American History

MULTIGENERATIONAL TRAUMA OCCURS FROM many sources: domestic violence, crime, infectious and life-threatening diseases, sexual abuse, drug abuse, loss of employment or loss of financial resources. People all over the world have been affected by the transmission of generational trauma at different times and in different ways. Survivors and families of war veterans; the children of military personnel missing in action; indigenous civilians of war torn countries such as Viet Nam, Palestine, Rwanda, Israel; victims of natural disasters such as Hurricane Katrina, the Haitian earthquake, the Japanese tsunami, and super storm Sandy; the Columbine, Virginia Tech, Sandy Hook, Baltimore, Charleston, Paris, and San Bernardino massacres are a few reminders of the constant presence of trauma in our lives.

Three events were selected, events affected by the transmission of generational trauma to study: The Jewish Holocaust of World War II, the Armenian Genocide of 1915, and the Native American Massacre at Wounded Knee of 1890. The Jewish Holocaust was selected because the children of the survivors of the Holocaust were the first population studied, and the findings prompted research of other populations. The Jewish Holocaust has a prominent awareness in the international community. In stark contrast, awareness of the Armenian Genocide of 1915 by the Turkish government is little known. With the compromised silence of the global community, Turkey continues to deny genocide happened in 1915. National pride, the association with Adolph Hitler and Nazi Germany, and the threat of sanction by the United Nations buttresses the Turkish government's refusal to acknowledge what happened as genocide.[1] There was interest in what differences there were, if any, in the behaviors of the children of the survivors of these two groups having such a sharp contrast in acknowledgment and publicity of their trauma.

With the Native American population, similarities were found with African Americans. They, like African Americans, were denied full expression of their culture, language, and religion. In a similar fashion, not by choice like the Jews and Armenians, Native Americans were restricted to preselected, destitute reservations similar in many ways to the segregated neighborhoods to which African Americans were confined. A major difference between the two groups is the loss of their homeland. Native Americans were not taken from their homeland like the Africans; their homeland was taken from them. Also, Native American spirituality is tied to the land, and their introduction to Christianity was through the Catholic Church. For African Americans, the evangelical Protestant church was the major influence in developing their spirituality. It raised the question were these factors influential in the ways generational trauma revealed itself in the descendants of the two groups?

INTERGENERATIONAL TRAUMA HISTORY

Intergenerational trauma was first noticed in 1966 by clinicians treating a high number of Canadian clients who were children of Holocaust survivors. Dr. Yael Danieli, a practicing clinical psychologist, traumatologist and victimologist, is the co-founder and director of the Group Project for Holocaust Survivors and their Children, and the founding director and former president of the International Society for Traumatic Stress Studies. She is also the editor of the *International Handbook of Multigenerational Legacies of Trauma*. In her introduction she writes:

> Multigenerational transmission of trauma is an integral part of human history. Transmitted in word, writing, body language, and even in silence, it is as old as humankind. It has been thought of, alluded to, written about, and examined in both oral and written histories in all societies, cultures, and religions.[2]

---

1. For further reference see Stanley, "A PBS Documentary."
2. Danieli, *International Handbook*, 1–2.

Part I

In 1980, Post-Traumatic Stress Disorder (PTSD), the concluding name given to the study of "survivor syndrome" was entered as a separate category in the Diagnostic and Statistical Manual of Mental Disorders (DSM-III). Since 1990, there have been studies of third and succeeding generations. Danieli and others advocated for the inclusion of intergenerational transmission of victimization-related trauma in DSM-5 published in 2013.[3]

Over the years the definition of trauma and its treatment have become more inclusive. Laura K. Jones and Jenny Cureton cite the changes since the first entry in the DSM-III.

> The examination of traumatic responses of combat and interpersonal violence led to the inclusion of a distinct PTSD diagnosis in the third edition of the DSM (DSM-III; APA, 1980) . . . The publications of the DSM-IV and DSM-IV-TR brought a considerably more inclusive definition of trauma (APA, 1994, 2000). Varied events as a car accident, a natural disaster, learning about a death of a loved one, and even a particularly difficult divorce were considered variations of traumatic experience . . . The 13 years between the *DSM-IV-TR* (2000) and the *DSM-5* (2013a) engendered considerable debate regarding how trauma was defined . . . In the *DSM-5*, PTSD now serves as the cornerstone of a new category of diagnoses, Trauma and Stress Related Disorder, (TSRD) . . . Exposure to a traumatic or aversive event is now recognized as a vital cause of an entire class of conditions affecting mental well-being . . . Several changes in the *DSM-5* definition stand out immediately, such as the inclusion of sexual violence within the core premise of trauma. Experiencing sexual violence may precipitate PTSD, as can witnessing it, learning about it and experiencing repeated exposure to stories of such acts . . . a new subset of possible exposure has been established, namely vicarious trauma. This is the first time that *DSM* criteria have included deleterious effects of repeatedly witnessing or hearing stories regarding the aftermath of trauma. This inclusion may not be surprising to trauma counselors, as nearly 15 to 20 percent develop PTSD symptoms from hearing and sharing in the stories of survivors . . . However, the *DSM-5* clearly states that vicarious trauma cannot be the result of repeated exposure via electronic or print media. This precludes, for example, McNally's (2009) case example of an individual with

---

3. Ibid., 3.

trauma symptoms who repeatedly witnessed the attacks on the World Trade Center by way of television monitors.[4]

Vicarious trauma, though not specifically identified as intergenerational trauma does acknowledge the destructive effects of hearing stories regarding the aftermath of trauma.

THE JEWISH HOLOCAUST

The Holocaust was the genocide of approximately six million European Jews throughout Nazi-occupied territory during World War II by Nazi Germany, led by Adolf Hitler. Of the nine million Jews who had resided in Europe before the Holocaust, approximately two-thirds perished: an estimated one million children, two million women, and three million men. Some scholars maintain that the definition of the Holocaust should also include Romani, communists, Soviet prisoners of war, Polish and Soviet civilians, homosexuals, people with disabilities, Jehovah's Witnesses, and other political and religious opponents, whether they were of German or non-German ethnic origin. Using this definition, the total number of Holocaust victims is between eleven and seventeen million.

Most historians claim that the civilian population was unaware of the war crimes that were carried out, especially in the extermination camps, which were located outside Germany in Nazi-occupied Europe. Historical evidence indicates that the vast majority of Holocaust victims were unaware of the fate that awaited them and believed they were to be resettled.[5]

Motivation for the Holocaust

The motivation for the Holocaust was antisemitism, ethnic cleansing (the elimination of "weaker undesirables") and Nazi propaganda of a Jewish Communist takeover. Hitler has been noted saying that the Armenian

---

4. Jones and Cureton, "Trauma Redefined," 257–71.

5. Ibid. For further reading see Holocaust Research Project, "Nazi Propaganda," www.holocaustresearchproject.org/holoprelude/nazprop.html; United States Holocaust Memorial Museum, "Propaganda," http://www.ushmm.org/propaganda/; Snyder, *Bloodlands*; Hedgepeth and Saidel, *Sexual Violence against Jewish Women*; Davies and Lukas, *The Forgotten Holocaust*; Wytwycky, *The Other Holocaust*.

PART I

Genocide and the lack of public outcry against it inspired his plan to purge the Jews from German society.[6]

Methods Used in the Holocaust

The persecution and genocide were carried out in stages. Initially various laws to remove the Jews from civil society, most prominently the Nuremberg Laws, were enacted in Nazi Germany years before the outbreak of World War II. Concentration camps were established in which inmates were subjected to slave labor until they died of exhaustion or disease. When Germany conquered new territory in eastern Europe, specialized units killed Jews and political opponents in mass shootings. The occupiers required Jews and Romani to be confined in overcrowded ghettos before being transported by freight train to extermination camps where, if they survived the journey, most were killed in gas chambers.[7]

Manifestation of Trauma

Danieli first researched multigenerational transmission of trauma with the children of Holocaust survivors in 1980. Her studies found they displayed depression, suicidal ideation and behavior, guilt and concern about betraying the ancestors for being excluded from the suffering, obligation to share in the ancestral pain, a sense of being obliged to take care of and be responsible for survivor parents, a sense of being obliged to compensate for the genocidal legacy, persecutory and intrusive memories of the Holocaust, as well as grandiose fantasies, dreams, images, and perception of the world as dangerous. She named the cluster of characteristics "survivor child complex."[8]

In these initial studies, Danieli identified four key concepts: the Conspiracy of Silence; Trauma and the Continuity of Self: A Multidimensional, Multidisciplinary Integrative Framework (TCMI); the Intergenerational Context; and Vulnerability and/or Resiliency.

---

6. Danieli, *International Handbook*, 206.
7. For further reading see Berenbaum, *The World Must Know*.
8. Danieli, *International Handbook*, 4.

Conspiracy of Silence

The first and most striking concept Danieli found was the conspiracy of silence. The survivors were not allowed to talk about their experiences. Even mental health professionals believed the survivors were too emotionally fragile to discuss what had happened to them. Denial, repression, avoidance, and indifference were the reactions by both the Jewish community and the larger society. The survivors were accused of actively or passively participating in their own destiny by "going like sheep to slaughter." "Bystander's guilt," accusations that nothing was done to stop the killings, led many to accuse the survivors of participating in immoral acts to survive. The bystanders wanted to forget; the survivors wanted to talk. Feeling the resistance and misunderstanding of their motives, the Holocaust survivors stopped talking, resulting in silence that exacerbated their loneliness, mistrust, and isolation.[9]

Trauma and the Continuity of Self: A Multidimensional, Multidisciplinary Integrative Framework (TCMI)

Danieli created a model to illustrate the complexity and interrelationship of systems that make up a person's identity. Some of the systems she ascertained were biological, spiritual, cultural, educational, economic, and political. These systems coexist dynamically along a time dimension which creates a perception of life from the past through the present and into the future. When these systems are exposed to trauma, she proposes, it causes a rupture in identity. She writes:

> Exposure to trauma causes a rupture, a possible regression, and a state of being "stuck" in this free flow, which Danieli calls *fixity*. The time, duration, extent, and meaning of the trauma for the individual, the survival mechanisms/strategies utilized to adapt to it (e.g., see Danieli, 1985), as well as post victimization traumata variously described as the conspiracy of silence (Danieli, 1985) . . . will determine the elements and degree of rupture, the disruption, disorganization, and disorientation, and the severity of the fixity. The fixity may render the individual vulnerable, particularly to further trauma/ruptures, throughout the life cycle. For example, the Nazi Holocaust not only ruptured continuity but also destroyed all the individual's existing supports. The ensuing,

9. Ibid., 4.

pervasive conspiracy of silence between survivors and society, including mental health professionals, deprived them and their children of potential supports (Danieli, 1985).[10]

Intergenerational Context

Viewed from a family systems perspective, what happened in one generation will affect what happens in the younger generation, though the actual behavior may take a variety of forms. Danieli described at least four differing postwar "adaptational styles" of Holocaust survivor families: Victim families, Fighter families, Numb families, and "Those who made it (successful)" families. She writes:

> The family is a carrier of conscious and unconscious values, myths, fantasies, and beliefs that may not be shared by the larger community or culture ... Different cultures capitalize on different pathways to acculturate their young. Thus, beyond the familial, from parents to offspring, entire bodies of human endeavor are vehicles of transmission: oral history, literature and drama, history and politics, religious ritual and writings, cultural traditions and the study thereof, such as anthropology, biology, and genetics. And the various disciplines examine, from their different perspectives, these identity dimensions.[11]

Vulnerability and/or Resilience

Danieli acknowledges the two different perspectives to retraumatization. The vulnerability perspective holds that trauma leaves permanent psychic damage that renders survivors more vulnerable when subsequently faced with extreme stress. The resilience perspective holds that coping well with initial trauma will strengthen resistance to the effects of future trauma. Material and human resources, personality, and predispositions play a large factor in how individuals cope with subsequent trauma.

> With survivors, it is especially hard to draw conclusions based on outward appearances. Survivors often display external markers of success (i.e. occupational achievement or establishing families)

10. Ibid., 5.
11. Ibid., 9–10.

that in truth represent survival strategies. However, there are also other facets of adaptation that are largely internal and intrapsychic.... Despite optimistic views of adaptation, even survivors in the "those who made it" category still experience difficulties related to their traumatic past, suggesting that overly optimistic views may describe defense rather than effective coping. In fact it is within this category that we observe the highest rates of suicide among survivors as well as their children.[12]

Coping Strategies

Holocaust survivors and their families retained their history, identity, and culture through their religion. Validation of their identity is nurtured by their faith from within the group. Establishing a homeland in 1948 and renewing their language strengthened their cultural identity. The insistence on commemorations of the event, i.e., "never forget," supporting each other economically, investing in their own communities, gaining economic, political and financial control, and assimilating "in the world but not of it" are additional coping strategies.

THE ARMENIAN GENOCIDE

Armenian History

Armenia is located in the southern Caucasus and is the smallest of the former Soviet republics. It is bounded by Georgia on the north, Azerbaijan on the east, Iran on the south, and Turkey on the west. Contemporary Armenia is a fraction of the size of ancient Armenia. One of the world's oldest civilizations, Armenia once included Mount Ararat, which biblical tradition identifies as the mountain where Noah's ark rested after the flood. It was the first country in the world to officially embrace Christianity as its religion (c. C.E. 300). Under Tigrane the Great (fl. 95–55 B.C.E.), the Armenian empire reached its height and became one of the most powerful in Asia, stretching from the Caspian to the Mediterranean seas.[13]

12. Ibid., 10.
13. See "The Origins." http://armenianhistory.info/chapter-i-the-origins/.

Part I

Throughout most of its history, Armenia was conquered by Greeks, Romans, Persians, Byzantines, Mongols, Arabs, Ottoman Turks and Russians. After the conquest of Constantinople by Sultan Mehmed II in 1453, Armenia was incorporated into the Ottoman Empire. From the beginning of the sixteenth century, Armenia became a scene of confrontation between the Ottoman Empire and Iran. Following the final armistice in 1639, the territory of Great Armenia was split in two. The Western Armenia fell to the Ottoman Empire, and the Eastern Armenia became part of Iran.

From the sixteenth century through World War I, major portions of Armenia were controlled by the Ottoman Turks, under whom the Armenians experienced discrimination, religious persecution, heavy taxation, and armed attacks. In response to Armenian nationalist stirrings, the Turks massacred thousands of Armenians in 1894 and 1896. The most horrific massacre took place in April 1915, during World War I, when the Turks ordered the deportation of the Armenian population to the deserts of Syria and Mesopotamia. According to the majority of historians, between 600,000 and 1.5 million Armenians were murdered or died of starvation. The Armenian massacre is considered the first genocide of the twentieth century. Turkey denies that genocide took place and claims that a much smaller number died in a civil war.

After the Turkish defeat in World War I, the independent Republic of Armenia was established in 1918, but survived only until 1920, when it was annexed by the Soviet army. In 1922, the Soviets joined Georgia, Armenia, and Azerbaijan to form the Transcaucasian Soviet Socialist Republic, which became part of the USSR. In 1936, after a reorganization, Armenia became a separate constituent republic of the USSR. Armenia declared its independence from the collapsing Soviet Union in 1991.[14]

Motivation for the Genocide

The historical situations culminating in the genocide of the Armenians and the destruction of the Jews resemble one another. Both groups were targeted because of their birth membership in a despised group, for their religion, and for their suspected alliance with the communist party.

---

14. Ibid.

Methods Used in the Genocide

As the power and influence of the Ottoman Empire began to shrink, the persecution of the Armenians increased. From 1895 to 1896, between 100 and 200,000 were killed or driven out of the Armenian provinces. In 1909, thirty thousand were killed. In 1915, the Turkish government decided to totally eliminate the Armenians. It was a systematic purging beginning with the Armenian soldiers, then the male community and religious leaders. The women, children, and elderly were either forced into slavery or onto death marches to the desert without food and water in order to weaken them so they would not try to escape, and to accelerate the death rate. Survival rates from the marches were very low. Out of 19,900 Armenians from the three towns of Sivas, Kharput, and Erzerum, only 361 reached the last stop before being driven into the desert, with unknown results. It is estimated that one and a half million Armenians perished between 1915 and 1923. The Turkish government hid the genocide as much as possible, and its successor governments have steadily denied it, with a disinformation effort that has grown progressively more forceful, sophisticated, and public in recent years.[15] An estimated 60 percent of all 8 million Armenians worldwide live outside the country, with 1 million each in the United States and Russia. Other significant Armenian communities are located in Georgia, France, Iran, Lebanon, Syria, Argentina, and Canada.[16]

Manifestations of Trauma

For reason of cultural and religious differences between the Armenian and Jewish community, "survivor's guilt" is a major manifestation in the Jewish community but not in the Armenian community. A comparison of the literature of both cultures shows remorseful guilt is absent from the Armenian literature. The commemorative function of guilt, which is to maintain a connection and loyalty to the deceased, may be absent because of the Armenian Christian belief in an afterlife and the community commemoration on April 24 of Armenian Martyrs' Day. Those who perished are regarded not as victims but as martyrs who died for their faith and their ethnic heritage.[17]

15. Kupelian et. al, "Turkish Genocide," 192–93.
16. Ibid.
17. Ibid.

PART I

Authors

Dr. Diane Kupelian is a clinical psychologist. She earned her B.A. from Vassar College, and her M.A. and Ph.D. from American University. She is President of the National Alliance of Mental Illness, Montgomery County, Maryland. Dr. Kupelian has published and lectured internationally on the effect of Post-Traumatic Stress Disorder on families. She has lectured for the International Society of Traumatic Stress Studies, the Scholars' Conference on the Churches and the Holocaust, and the Armenian American Association for the Study of Stress and Genocide.

Dr. Anie Sanentz-Kalayjian is a professor of Psychology at Fordham University and the founder and co-director of the Association for Trauma Outreach and Prevention. She is recognized as an international expert on the psychological effect of trauma on disaster victims. Her most recent publication is *Forgiveness and Reconciliation: Psychological Pathways to Conflict Transformation and Peace Building*.

Dr. Alice Kassabian (1926–2011) was a clinical social worker, and founding member and former president of the Greater Washington Society for Clinical Social Work. She had a private practice in Northern Virginia and was an adjunct professor in the School of Social Work at Virginia Commonwealth University.

Kupelian, Sanentz-Kalayjian, Kassabian quote researchers Drs. Levon Boyajian and Haigaz Grigorian.[18] In their study of psychosocial damage of the genocide, they found symptoms among Armenian survivors that are similar to those of the Jewish Holocaust including:

> anxiety, depression, compulsive associations to trauma-related material, guilt, nightmares, irritability, emptiness, fear of loving and inability to experience pleasure from activities usually found enjoyable e.g. hobbies, exercise, sports, social activities. Salerian (1982) adds phobias, psychosomatic disorders, and severe personality changes Second generation participants in the study by (Boyajian and Grigorian 1988) reported manifestations of anxiety in association with extreme parental overprotectiveness. Anger and frustration for all generations were associated with the denial of the genocide by the Turkish government. They felt alienated and

---

18. For further reading Boyajian and Grigorian, "Sequelae"; Boyajian and Grigorian, "Psychological Sequelae"; Salerian, "A Psychological Report."

dishonored, their suffering pointless and see it as a psychological continuation of the genocide, and a continuing victimization.[19]

Another factor that differs between the Jewish and Armenian survivors is that the "conspiracy of silence" found in the Jewish community was internal between the survivors and those who did not experience it. The silence left the Holocaust survivors profoundly rebuffed, alienated and mistrustful. It sustained their silence and impeded their ability to mourn, integrate, and heal; it isolated them from others, including other Jews who had not shared their experience. The "conspiracy of silence" for the Armenians was different. It came from outside the community. The silence did not tend to create a chasm within the Armenian community because the genocide had affected virtually all Armenians. The silence invalidated the entire community.[20]

Coping Strategies

Several factors historically supported a coherent and persistent sense of Armenian ethnic identity within the Ottoman context. First, the Armenians' ancient origins and the preservation of their historic territory until World War I gave them a sense of who they were in their own homeland. Second, the Armenian language was distinct from that of surrounding people. Third, the unique Armenian Church has remained a central cultural unifying factor for 2000+ years. Fourth was the Millet system of religious self-government within the Ottoman Empire.

In 1987, Alice Kassabian conducted a study of three generations of families and found a clear commitment to ethnic identity, suggesting the families were able to protect and transmit that identity. All three generations desired to maintain social contact in the Armenian community; to teach their children Armenian history, culture, and traditions; and to give their children Armenian language lessons. The three generations shared a similar perception of the family environment suggesting that they share a mutual set of values. There is very strong community cohesion. Each generation in its own way opposed the intended outcome of annihilation and unified the Armenian community to withstand the impact. By living with Armenian self-awareness, each family has transmitted this opposition

---

19. Kupelian et. al, "Turkish Genocide," 194.
20. Ibid., 195.

from generation to generation. Also Turkey's active, ongoing denial of their victimization may have created an abiding anger that overshadows any experience of guilt for surviving and prospering. The active Turkish denial has provided the psychological oppositional pressure that has maintained the effect of a persistent ethnic identity.[21]

THE NATIVE AMERICAN MASSACRE AT WOUNDED KNEE, SOUTH DAKOTA

The Ghost Dance spiritual movement's message was that Native Americans had been defeated and confined to reservations because they had angered the gods by abandoning their traditional customs. In a desperate attempt to return to the days of their glory, many sought salvation in a new mysticism preached by a Paiute shaman called Wovoka. Emissaries from the Sioux in South Dakota traveled to Nevada to hear his words. Many Sioux believed that if they practiced the Ghost Dance and rejected the ways of the white man, the gods would create the world anew and destroy all non-believers, including non-Indians. On December 15, 1890, reservation police tried to arrest Sitting Bull, the famous Sioux chief, who they mistakenly believed was a Ghost Dancer. They killed him in the process, increasing the tensions at Pine Ridge, South Dakota.

On December 29, the U.S. Army's 7th Cavalry surrounded a band of Ghost Dancers under Big Foot, a Lakota Sioux chief, near Wounded Knee Creek and demanded they surrender their weapons. A fight broke out between an Indian and a U.S. soldier and a shot was fired. In the confusion, who fired the first shot was not determined. A brutal massacre followed, in which an estimated 150 Indians were killed (some historians put this number at twice as high), nearly half of them women and children. After a blizzard, the cavalry returned on January 1, 1891 and buried the frozen bodies in a mass grave.

Motivation for Massacre

Some historians speculate that the soldiers of the 7th Cavalry were deliberately taking revenge for the regiment's defeat at the Battle of Little Bighorn, led by George Custer in 1876. Other motivations could include the

21. Ibid.

discovery of gold in the Black Hills, occupation of land, and fear of the Ghost Dance religious movement. "Whatever the motives, the massacre ended the Ghost Dance movement and was the last major confrontation in America's deadly war against the Plains Indians."[22]

Manifestation of Trauma

Dr. Maria Yellow Horse Brave Heart is the president and director/cofounder of the Takini Network of Rapid City, South Dakota and an associate research professor at the University of New Mexico. Brave Heart is a lateral descendant of Sitting Bull and a member of the White Lance extended family kinship network who are Wounded Knee descendants.

Brave Heart became conscious of her own unresolved historical trauma in 1978, and began incorporating the concept of historical legacy, later describing it as intergenerational Post Traumatic Stress Disorder (PTSD) in clinical work as well as community training and healing workshops. In 1988, she developed the theoretical construct of the historical trauma response. Confirmation of her experience among the Lakota and other Native people in clinical social work practice and community workshops, led to more systematic studies of historical trauma and its application in prevention and intervention."[23]

> The Lakota "historical trauma response" is analogous to the "survivor syndrome" and "survivor's child complex" identified among those who endured the Jewish Holocaust, and their progeny (Fogelman, 1988; Kestenberg, 1990; Niederland, 1988), and similar traits in other trauma survivors and descendants (Lifton 1988; Nagata, 1991; van der Kolk, 1987). Specific features of this historical trauma response include (a) transposition (Kestenberg, 1990) where one lives simultaneously in the past and the present with the ancestral suffering as the main organizing principal in one's life, (b) identification with the dead (Lifton, 1968, 1988) so that one feels psychically (emotionally and psychologically) dead and feels unworthy of living, and (c) maintaining loyalty to and identification with the suffering of deceased ancestors, re-enacting affliction within one's own life (Fogelman, 1988, 1991). Additionally, there

---

22. "Massacre at Wounded Knee, 1890," http://www.eyewitnesstohistory.com/knee.htm.

23. Brave Heart, "Wakiksuyapi," 247.

is survivor guilt, an ensuing fixation to trauma, reparatory fantasies, and attempts to undo the tragedy of the past.

Manifestations of the historical trauma response include depression, self-destructive behavior, psychic numbing, poor affect tolerance, anger, and elevated mortality rates from suicide and cardiovascular diseases observed among Jewish Holocaust survivors and descendants (Eitinger & Strom, 1973; Keehn, 1980; Sigal & Weinfeld, 1989) as well as among the Lakota (Brave Heart, 1998, 1999b; Brave Heart-Jordan, 1995). Lakota mortality rates for heart disease are almost two times the rate for the general United States population; suicide rates are more than twice the national average (Indian Health Service, 1995). The association of heart disease with PTSD and other psychiatric conditions such as depression has been identified by Hamner (1994) and Shapiro (1996). Current lifespan trauma, superimposed upon a traumatic ancestral past, creates additional challenges for Lakota survivors. The pervasiveness and frequency of traumatic exposure among modern American Indian youth is identified by Jones, Dauphinais, Sack, and Somervell (1997) and Manson, Beals, O'Nell, Piasecki, Bechtold, Keane, and Jones (1996).[24]

The Concept of Wakiksuyapi

Traditional Lakota culture encourages maintenance of a connection with the spirit world. The Lakota are predisposed to identification with ancestors from their historical past. Traditional mourning such as cutting the bereaved's hair and body are expressions of a felt loss of part of oneself with the death of a close relative. Grief was impaired due to massive losses across generations and the federal government's prohibition of indigenous practices for mourning resolution. These circumstances, impaired grief and proclivity for connection with the deceased, fueled *historical unresolved grief*, a component of the historical trauma response.[25]

Family members among Jewish Holocaust descendants who shoulder the collective generational trauma of lost ancestors are called "Memorial Candles." For the Lakota, the closeness of the extended kinship network and the degree of bereavement may

---

24. Ibid.
25. Ibid.

result in Wakiksuyapi or Memorial People, those who carry the grief and whose lives are a testimony to the lost ancestors. Carrying Lakota ancestral trauma may be extended to certain families, extended kinship networks or even bands. For example, following the assassination of Sitting Bull, many traumatized Hunkpapa (a band within the Lakota group) fled to join the Hohwoju, who mourned his death as if he were a near relative. These Hunkpapa and Hohwoju (a band within the Lakota group), led by Bigfoot, were pursued by the cavalry and massacred at Wounded Knee two weeks later. Settlement and intermarriage of many Hunkpapa and Hohwoju survivors among the Oglala, a band of Lakota, have placed these three bands at special risk for unresolved grief and trauma responses. Additionally, other Lakota and Dakota bands, because of their own traumatic histories and intermarriage with the Hunkpapa and Hohwoju, may also carry this particular historical legacy of trauma and unresolved grief. These are the Wakiksuyapi, true to the cultural mores around grief and the connection with the spirit world, who are shouldering cumulative massive generational trauma.[26]

Coping Strategies

Emergent themes from the data supported the theory of a Lakota historical trauma response. Ideas about healing and coping emphasized traditional Lakota values, particularly compassion and generosity, a collective survivor identity, and a commitment to traditionally oriented values and healing.

Brave Heart offers the historical trauma intervention model, which includes four major community intervention components: 1) confronting the historical trauma, 2) understanding the trauma, 3) releasing the pain of historical trauma, and 4) transcending the trauma. It also includes three major hypotheses for the intervention model: 1) education increases awareness of trauma, 2) sharing effects of trauma provides relief, and 3) grief resolution through collective mourning/healing creates positive group identity and commitment to community.[27]

26. Ibid., 248.
27. Ibid.

Part I

SIMILARITIES AND DIFFERENCES

In studying these three groups both similarities and differences were discovered in the motivations for the genocide, the perceptions by the "other," the importance of land, religion and spirituality, the significance of silence, and the retention of identity, culture, and history.

The Jews were perceived as impure and specifically persecuted for their religious beliefs. Until 1948, the Jews did not have an official homeland since the Jewish Roman Wars in 136 CE.[28] After the war, they migrated to northern and eastern Europe, North Africa or stayed in Babylon (present day Iraq). Since the Holocaust, they have preserved their culture, history, and identity through the framework of their religion. Their validation was internal; they affirmed themselves. They maintained a connection with their ancestors and with their children through their religious practices. There is a public communal acknowledgment and mourning for those who were killed. Silence was self-imposed in the Jewish community. Survivor's guilt played a large role in suppressing the trauma until therapy revealed a pattern of behaviors and attitudes that have been instrumental in helping other groups identify transgenerational trauma in their families. The Jewish Holocaust survivors and their children were able to benefit from family systems therapy that may not have been as available and widespread as when the Armenian Genocide happened thirty years earlier.

Silence was and still is the galvanizing force that strengthens the Armenian identity. The denial by the Turkish government, whose motivation appears to be avoidance of political shame, has been instrumental in the Armenian community's determination to hold onto its culture, language, and religious beliefs. The Armenians' Christian heritage has been the source of their persecution and their strength as a group. They did not experience survivor's guilt like the Jews because they all felt and still feel persecuted; no one was exempt. In the same way as the Jews, they were forced to leave their homeland and disperse to other countries. But unlike the Jews, they and their culture were not known or understood in the countries to which they migrated. Therefore, they had to create tightly knit communities in order to survive. Within their religious tradition and their community they also have a public and communal mourning of lives lost in the genocide.

The Massacre at Wounded Knee was the culmination of the tension between the United States and the Plains Native Americans. Even though

---

28. Eck, "The Bar Kokhba Revolt," 76–89.

they were considered by the American settlers to be savages, the fight was over land—the homeland and source of spirituality for the Native American. There was no diaspora for the Native Americans, but rather a confinement to land that was considered worthless. If the land was later found to have value such as gold, then they would be moved to another location. Unlike the Jews and Armenians, there was a concerted effort to destroy their culture, community, and faith. The intentional removal of children from families, the banning of their native language and participation in cultural traditions, substituting Catholicism for their own religious beliefs and traditions have had devastating effect on the Native American community. For Native Americans, the loss of their religious traditions and limited mobility have displayed in what Brave Heart has named historical unresolved grief.

Chapter 3

Generational Trauma in African American History

CHATTEL SLAVERY ENDED TWENTY-FIVE years before the Massacre at Wounded Knee; fifty-eight years before the Armenian Genocide and eighty years before the Jewish Holocaust. Depending on the starting point—1619, when the first Africans landed at Old Point Comfort (Fort Monroe) in Hampton, VA[1] and worked as indentured servants, or 1640, when John Punch, a runaway African indentured servant became the first African servant sentenced to servanthood for life, becoming the first documented slave—chattel slavery lasted between 225 and 246 years, approximately eight generations. An estimated 12 million Africans were captured and embarked on the slave ships, and an estimated 10.7 million arrived alive in North and South America. Even after slavery was outlawed by Britain in 1808, three million Africans were captured, and 2.6 million survived the Middle Passage. Of that 12 million captured, 26 percent (2.6 million) were children. Ninety percent of Africans were taken to South America because of the large number needed for the sugar plantations.[2]

The enslaved Africans were exposed to eight traumatic incidents: capture, forced march from the interior of the continent, the slave dungeons, the Middle Passage, separation and sale at auction, harsh plantation life, forced breeding, and daily threat of terrorism. The journey from capture to the castles sometimes took months, and time spent in the slave castles varied from one month to one year. The average time across the Atlantic

---

1 Project 1619, "The Landing Site," http://www.project1619.org/9.html.
2. Eltis and Richardson, *Atlas of the Transatlantic Slave Trade*, 19, 27.

was two months. In the Caribbean, they were sent to seasoning camps. Seasoning was a process conducted during the Atlantic slave trade for the purpose of "breaking" slaves. It took away the slaves' identities in order to make them passive and docile. During the seasoning process, the slaves would sometimes have hot tar and oil poured onto their sores and wounds. The Africans were kept in the camps from one to four years. The Africans taken to North America most often bypassed this treatment.[3]

In North America, the Africans were taken from the ships and held in holding pens until auction. Once on the plantation, the Africans were ill-fed and raggedly clothed and worked under extreme psychological and physical conditions, constantly under the threat of terrorist attacks, death, physical, and sexual abuse. When the British made the slave trade illegal in 1808, the slaveholders began breeding the enslaved. The United States imported less than 4 percent (an estimated 388,747) of the total number of Africans deported from Africa to the Americas and the Caribbean. However, in 1860, the United States had 3,954,000 enslaved people, the largest number of people of African descent ever assembled in the New World.[4]

Dr. Elaine Pinderhughes, a retired professor from Boston School of Social Work wrote in her article, "The Multigenerational Transmission of Loss and Trauma: The African American Experience":

> They [African Americans] are the only group whose immigration was wrought by force, under unthinkable brutal conditions, and whose subsequent existence was determined by legalized inequality. The consequent confluence of conditions under which they have been forced to live has exerted an ongoing and unrelentingly disruptive and traumatic effect upon their efforts to build cohesive families and communities to ensure their survival. From their arrival 400 years ago to the present day, their existence has been marked by massive and repetitive losses. As a result, the family and the community, the social institutions most significant to human survival have been in perpetual peril.[5]

Proof of this trauma-afflicted existence is revealed in many social indicators of the quality of current African American life: the high rate of poverty, marital disruption, single-parent families, incarceration, drug and alcohol abuse, homelessness, poor school achievement and high dropout

---

3. For further reading see Kiple, *Caribbean Slave*.
4. Eltis and Richardson, *Atlas of the Transatlantic Slave Trade*, 19, 27.
5. Pinderhughes, "The Multigenerational Transmission," 161.

rates, children in foster care, and disparities in health morbidity and mortality. These facts are the culminating results of generations of accrued deprivation, distress and transmission of racial tension.[6]

Vamik Volkan, a psychoanalyst and retired professor of psychiatry at the University of Virginia, developed the concept of transgenerational transmission of trauma. He postulates that members of communal groups who endure shameful and humiliating losses and traumas at the hands of enemy groups will continue, in an attempt to relieve their suffering, to transmit their "memories" of pain to subsequent generations. Volkan observes that:

> When a whole society has undergone massive trauma, victimized adults may endure guilt and shame for not having protected their children. The by-product of such trauma is a perennial, collective mourning over the loss of group dignity, self-esteem and identity. The mourning is characterized by conscious and unconscious communications passed down to generations in an attempt to mourn the group's losses and remove the collective sense of victimization. . . . As transgenerational transmissions of trauma occur, the trauma is perpetuated as its shared mental representation and is deposited into the psyches of subsequent generations, thereby impacting future generations with the same sense of helplessness, shame and humiliation experienced by the elders. Ultimately, the large group shares a collective identity which is perpetually haunted and stifled by its "memories" of victimization . . . If a sense of relief is to be found, the mourning related to the losses and trauma must be worked through, and the humiliation must be reversed.[7]

Established by Congress in 2000, the National Child Traumatic Stress Network (NCTSN) brings a singular and comprehensive focus to childhood trauma. NCTSN's collaboration of frontline providers, researchers, and families is committed to raising the standard of care while increasing access to services. Combining knowledge of child development, expertise in the full range of child traumatic experiences, and dedication to evidence-based practices, the NCTSN changes the course of children's lives by changing the course of their care. Their mission is to raise the standard of care

---

6. Institute for Research on Poverty, "FAQs about poverty," http://www.irp.wisc.edu/faqs/faq7.htm.

7. Scott, "A Perennial Mourning," 2.

and improve access to services for traumatized children, their families, and communities throughout the United States.[8]

As part of a Child Welfare Trauma Training Toolkit, fourteen types of trauma experienced by children in the United States are defined: sexual abuse or assault; physical abuse or assault; emotional abuse/psychological maltreatment; neglect (physical, medical, educational); serious accident (unintentional injury) or illness or extremely painful or life threatening medical procedure; witness to domestic violence; victim or witness to community violence; school violence; natural or manmade disasters; forced displacement; war/terrorism/political violence; victim/witness to extreme personal or interpersonal violence (intended to include exposure to homicide, suicide, and other similar extreme events); traumatic grief or separation; and system induced trauma (traumatic removal from the home, sibling separation or multiple placements in a short time).

A minimum of eight trauma types can be correlated to each of the eight trauma events in the Africans' journey from their homes to the plantations in the Americas (see appendix C). All of the trauma events: capture, forced march from the interior of the continent, the slave castles, the Middle Passage, auction, plantation life, breeding, and terrorism, could happen to one African in twelve months.[9]

Revisiting Ouobna Ottobah Cugoano's narrative identifies several of the trauma types from his capture to his arrival in Grenada. He was "snatched away" from his home while playing in the fields with eighteen to twenty boys and girls. The first devastating event was the capture—an abrupt, unexplained and/or indefinite separation from a parent, primary caretaker, or sibling due to circumstances beyond the child victim's control which would cause traumatic grief and separation from his home and family. The second overwhelming event is forced displacement due to war/terrorism/political reasons. Cugoano describes what he saw: "The horrors I soon saw and felt, cannot be well described; I saw many of my miserable countrymen chained two and two, some handcuffed, and some with their hands tied behind."[10] The third disastrous event was victim/witness

8. The National Child Traumatic Stress Network, "Trauma Types," http://www.nctsn.org/trauma-types.

9. The trauma definitions identified by the National Child Traumatic Stress Network events can be related to capture, forced march, imprisonment in the slave castle, the middle passage, the auction, plantation life of rape and physical abuse, separation of families, chronic institutionalize oppression and terrorism.

10. Cugoano, *Narrative of the Enslavement*, 121–24.

Part I

to extreme personal/interpersonal violence by or between individuals, and physical abuse actual or attempted infliction of physical pain with or without use of an object or weapon, and including use of severe corporeal punishment. Cugoano's description of the Middle Passage points out several traumas added to this calamitous narrative:

> But when a vessel arrived to conduct us away to the ship, it was a most horrible scene; there was nothing to be heard but the rattling of chains, smacking of whips, and the groans and cries of our fellow-men and a plan was concerted amongst us, that we might burn and blow up the ship, and to perish all together in the flames: but we were betrayed by one of our own countrywomen, who slept with some of the headmen of the ship, for it was common for the dirty filthy sailors to take the African women and lie upon their bodies; but the men were chained and pent up in holes. It was the women and boys which were to burn the ship, with the approbation and groans of the rest; though that was prevented, the discovery was likewise a cruel bloody scene.[11]

Like Cugoano, approximately eight generations of Africans were exposed to the trauma of unwanted or coercive sexual contact or exposure; deprivation of food, clothing and shelter; emotional abuse; forced displacement; physical abuse; traumatic grief, and separation before they arrived in North and South America.[12] The trauma types defined by the NCTSN do not consider the disruption of language, religious beliefs, diet, weather, and disease. The first four traumatic episodes: capture, forced march, the slave castles, and the Middle Passage were experienced by all who came from Africa. Once they arrived, the trauma continued with the fragmentation of the family through the auction, the hard labor of plantation life, breeding, and sustained terrorism. Carrying the traumas of their African ancestors, and with the memory of their homeland and families fading with each generation born in America, the black people who were born in America lived between two worlds—no longer African but not American. Negotiating the slave master's world was a matter of life and death. It meant learning the language and anticipating the expectations, walking the razor's edge knowing one mistake, actual or imagined, could mean a beating, maiming, branding, raping or death.

---

11. Ibid.
12. Klein, *Atlantic Slave Trade*, 178.

Generational Trauma in African American History

The most devastating trauma the "American born" enslaved people endured was the sale and separation of family. Three converging circumstances fostered this disruptive practice: the end of the international slave trade in 1808, the decrease in demand for labor in Virginia, Delaware and Maryland (the Upper South)[13] and the westward expansion for new land required because tobacco farming exhausted the land in the Upper South. The Upper South shifted from tobacco farming to breeding and trading enslaved people to meet the new demand as planters moved further south and west. Michael Tadman writes in *Speculators and Slaves: Masters, Traders, and Slaves in the Old South*:

> We should note, first, there has never been any real doubt that the antebellum period saw a massive interregional movement of slaves. In fact, between the years 1820 and 1860, the movement averaged, each decade some 200,000 (or fully 10 percent of the Upper South's slave population) were sold from the Upper South to the Lower South and West . . . Although the trade of people from north to south and west brought the most disruption, it is important to be aware that separation also occurred *within* states and regions.[14]

While doing research in black newspapers that began publication after the Civil War, Dr. Heather Williams, author of *Help Me to Find My People*, noticed advertisements of African Americans searching for family members who had been sold in slavery. Williams found over 1200 "Information Wanted" or "Lost Friends" advertisements between 1860 and 1870. Two examples were written in the *Colored Tennessean* in Nashville one week apart, six months after the end of the Civil War. On October 7, 1865, Thornton Copeland is trying to find his mother. He had been sold away from her twenty-one years earlier. His advertisement reads:

> Information is wanted of my mother, whom I left in Fauquier County, VA, in 1844, and I was sold in Richmond, VA., to Saml. Copeland. I formerly belonged to Robert Rogers. I am very anxious to hear from my mother and any information in relation to her whereabouts will be very thankfully received. My mother's name was Betty, and was sold by Col. Briggs to James French.—Any

---

13. Berlin, *Many Thousand Gone*, 262–68.
14. Tadman, *Speculators and Slaves*, 5.

PART I

> information by letter addressed to the Colored Tennessean, Box 1150, will be thankfully received.[15]

On October 14, 1865, Charity Moss placed an advertisement looking for her two sons:

> Information is wanted of my two boys, James and Horace, one of whom was sold in Nashville and the other was sold in Rutherford County. I, myself, was sold in Nashville and sent to Alabama, by Wm. Boyd. I and my children belonged to David Moss, who was connected with the Penitentiary in some capacity. Charity Moss
> P.S. Any information sent to Colored Tennessean office, Box 1150 will be thankfully received.[16]

These sales undermined marriage and family. The slave master repeatedly sabotaged men's roles as provider and protector for their families. The assault on gender roles left deep scars in the relationship between the enslaved men and women. The women were sexually abused, and when becoming pregnant, suffered many miscarriages. If they were able to carry their pregnancy to term, they often grieved the loss of their babies dying as infants. Health care was administered to stabilize or increase production of work. The enslaved people were forced to be dependent, submissive, fearful of their masters, and to regard themselves as inferior. Total obedience and absolute control were the order of the day.

In *Unchained Memories: Reading From The Slave Narratives*, a collection of slave narratives, the pain and devastation of the disruption of the family can be heard.

The Auction

> Talkin' 'bout somethin' awful, you should have been dere. De slave owners was shoutin' and sellin' chillen to one man and de mama and pappy to 'nother. De slaves cries and takes on somethin' awful. If a woman had lots of chillen she was sold for mo, 'cause it a sign she a good breeder.—Millie Williams, Texas[17]

> I was growed up when the war com, an' I was a mother befo' it closed. Babies was snatched from dere mother's breas' an' sold to speculators. Chilluns was separated from sisters an' brothers an'

---

15. Fleischner, *Mastering Slavery*, 1.
16. Ibid., 2.
17. Gates, *Unchained Memories*, 28.

never saw each other ag'in. Course dey cry; you think dey not cry when they was sold lak cattle? I could tell you 'bout it all day, but even den you couldn't guess the awfulness of it. I never seed none of my brothers an' sisters 'cept brother William. Him an' my mother an' me was brought in a speculator's drove to Richmon' an' put in a warehouse wid a drove of other niggas. Den we was all put on a block an' sol' to de highes' bidder.—Delia Garlic, Alabama[18]

Neglect

If I had my life to live over I would die fighting rather than be a slave again. I want no man's yoke on my shoulders no more. They didn't half feed us either. They fed the animals better. They gives the mules, ruffage and such, to chaw on all night. But they didn't give us nothing to chaw on. Learned us to steal, that's what they done. Why we would take anything we could lay our hands on, when we was hungry. Then they'd whip us for lieing when we say we don't know nothing about it. But it was easier to stand, when the stomach was full.—Robert Falls, Tennessee[19]

Physical Abuse

Dey way dey whip de niggers was to strip 'em off naked and whip 'em till dey make blisters and bus' de blisters. Den dey take de salt and red pepper and put in de wounds. After dey wash and grease dem and put somethin' on dem from bleed to death.—Sarah Ashely, Texas[20]

Sexual Abuse

My mother's mistress had three boys, one twenty-one, one nineteen, and one seventeen. Old mistress had gone away to spend the day one day. Mother always worked in the house. She did't work on the farm in Missouri. While she was alone, the boys came in and threw her down on the floor and tied her down so she couldn't struggle, and one after the other used her as long as they wanted for the whole afternoon. Mother was sick when her mistress came home. When old mistress wanted to know what was the matter with her, she told her what the boys had done. She whipped them and that's they way I came here.—Mary Estes Peters, Arkansas[21]

18. Ibid., 34.
19. Ibid., 101.
20. Ibid., 96.
21. Ibid.

Part I

The trauma of the enslaved African Americans caused them to have an inner life of repeated fear and terror, death anxiety, psychic numbing, disconnection, and isolation. The shock, misery, and abuse of chattel slavery precipitated an interior existence of enduring horror, emotional paralysis, and disassociation. The psychophysical experience of serious threat and injury created by abandonment, aggression, and betrayal created frightening thoughts, painful emotions, and physical distress in these tyrannized human beings. "Soul murder," a term coined by psychiatrist Leonard Shengold,[22] refers to violent and/or sexual abuse which presents children with too much sensation to bear, and neglect that deprives children of enough attention to meet their psychic needs. In studying the traumatized enslaved women who suffered sexual abuse from slave masters and physical, verbal, and emotional abuse from slave mistresses, historian Nell Painter identifies the manifestations of "soul murder" in their lives as low self-esteem, anger, and identification with the aggressor.[23]

Joy DeGruy has developed a term similar to "soul murder." She defines Post Traumatic Slave Syndrome (PTSS) as a condition that exists when a population has experienced multigenerational trauma resulting from 1) centuries of slavery, 2) continued experiences of oppression, 3) institutionalized racism, and 4) belief (real or imagined) that the benefits of the society in which they live are not accessible to them.[24] A syndrome is a particular set of behaviors and emotions that are brought about by a distinct set of circumstances. Multigenerational trauma, plus continued oppression, minus opportunity to access the benefits available in the society leads to PTSS. DeGruy defines three categories of behavior in her definition of PTSS: 1) vacant esteem, 2) ever present anger, and 3) racist socialization. Vacant esteem is believing oneself to have little or no value. This belief is formed by messages of inferiority from family, community, and the larger society. Signs of vacant esteem are melancholy, pessimism, jealousy, envy, and depression.

Anger and violence were molded into every aspect of slavery. Any group of people living under such harsh conditions will learn the ways of their captors. This learned behavior is aggravated by the accumulated generational frustration of false promises and blocked opportunities and goals.

---

22 For further reading see Shengold, *Soul Murder*.
23. Painter, *Soul Murder and Slavery*, 5.
24. DeGruy Leary, *Post Traumatic Slave Syndrome*, 119.

At any time, at any point, on any occasion, the anger can erupt, triggered by a perceived or real injustice.

Racist socialization is the adoption of the oppressor/aggressor's value system: white is superior, and black is inferior. Standards of beauty and material success are imitated. Glamorizing thug life, sexual promiscuity, lack of education, and selecting sports and entertainment as primary avenues of achievement reinforce the prejudice of whites.

RESILIENCE AND RESISTANCE

Resilience is the ability to adapt to difficult or challenging life experiences wherein a person overcomes adversity, and recovers from disruptive change or misfortune in order to thrive under extreme, on-going pressure without acting in dysfunctional or harmful ways. Resistance is the refusal to accept or comply with persons, situations or institutions wherein a person uses action or argument to oppose legal, political, economic, social, and spiritual injustice. It is evident that both resilience and resistance were active in the lives of enslaved men, women and children.

Janoff-Bulmam in *Shattered Assumptions* cites three beliefs that are commonly fractured by trauma: life is fair; people are generally good; and life is good and predictable. The enslaved people were forced to endure a fragmented existence in which their reality was inequitable, discriminatory, and prejudiced; people were sadistic, barbaric, and ruthless, and their circumstances were mercurial, whimsical, and turbulent. Chronic deprivation, distress and destitution insist a reassessment of fundamental values and priorities. People will become less materialistic and more relationship oriented. Nell Painter points out two components of resilience operating in the lives of the enslaved: 1) a countervailing value system of family, fictive kinship, and a "female slave network" and 2) a countervailing belief system promising equity and justice would ultimately prevail in the world of God.[25]

Even in the oppressive atmosphere of slavery, there were ways in which the enslaved found comfort and support within their community. In the evening after a day's work, away from the eyes of overseers, they squeezed in a few hours to nurture their children, exchange important information about plans for escape, to sing and tell stories, and to talk and laugh. It was during this time that they validated each other and acknowledged each other's value as human beings. They created a value system

25. Painter, *Soul Murder and Slavery*, 22.

PART I

that counterbalanced the invalidation of the slave masters. These were the moments they cherished and held on to during the day. The private times together allowed them to express their emotions, their grief over the loss or abuse of a loved one, or their joy of loving someone. Depending on the temperament of the slave master, there could be weddings, Christmas parties and Saturday night parties. Wash Ingram, an emancipated slave from Texas describes parties on their plantation:

> Saturday night, we would have parties and dance and play ring games. We had de parties dere in a big double log house. Dey would give us whiskey and wine and cherry brandy, but dere wasn' no shootin' or gamblin.' Dey didn' 'lowit. De men and women didn' do like dey do now. If dey had such carryin's on as dey do now, de white folks would have whipped 'em good.[26]

Christmas and New Year's Day were bittersweet because New Year's Day was auction day. In her biography *Incidents in the Life of a Slave Girl*, Harriet Jacobs (under the pen name of Linda Brent) recalled how they were given several days to celebrate because the first day of the new year always brought an auction. The night watch service that became a tradition in the African American church began as enslaved people prayed on New Year's Eve not to be sold. Based on oral tradition, Mrs. Corine Cannon, Dr. Katie G. Cannon's mother, was told by her grandmother, Mary Lytle, that people were selected to be sold on July 4th. They would then be separated from the rest to be prepared for sale on New Year's Day. They received better food and health care in order to bring a higher price at the auction, and on New Year's Day they would be sold.

In situations when individuals are totally powerless, faith in a greater power than self becomes a compelling means of survival. In *Soul Theology*, Cooper-Lewter and Mitchell identify the core beliefs African Americans have about God and themselves as a Christian community. These beliefs sustained the enslaved and their descendants and gave them the resilience to withstand the horrors of slavery.[27]

Hope is the expectation, anticipation, wish, longing, dream of justice, equality, and fairness in order to create wholeness, freedom, healing, peace, and well-being. It takes courage to move into the inner pain of loss or trauma. Hope is the belief that in spite of the pain, it will be better on the other side, and that healing is found by going through the pain.

26. Gates, *Unchained Memories*, 117.
27. Cooper-Lewter and Mitchell, *Soul Theology*, xi.

Two themes were prominent in the theology of the slaves: impending judgement punishing the wicked and rewarding the good, and Jesus' concern for the oppressed and the repudiation of the hierarchies of this world. Their theology was grounded in the belief that God is in charge. When life looks pretty bad, when one door is shut, God reserves the right to open another one. God is just—no oppression goes unpunished and no sacrificial suffering goes unnoticed and unrewarded. God's power works in the present situation. The God of the universe knows when and how to exercise God's might to relieve stressful situations and keep life within bearable bounds. One of the songs sung by the enslaved people was "My God is writing all the time . . . He sees all you do, an' he hears all you say, my God is writing all the time." They believed God was a God of mercy. No wrongdoing (sin) renders one unacceptable if one takes responsibility for the wrongdoing (confession) and commits to change the attitude, behavior, etc. (repentance).

The enslaved peoples' theology included core beliefs about themselves, their relationship to each other, and to God. They were children of God, made in God's image and equal in God's sight. They belonged to the family of God. The reality of permanent separation of family made this belief of significant importance. It functioned in creating a "new" family that went beyond the bloodlines. They were brothers and sisters in Christ. As members of a larger family held together spiritually, they could bear each other's burdens. They could persevere and endure and not give up in despair.

The slave master tried to control and subdue this theology by having both white and enslaved preachers preach a message of submissiveness. Secret gatherings at night, out of the view and earshot of slaveholders, gave them the opportunity to worship in a manner that was more meaningful to them, and it was an important survival tool.

Baby Suggs' sermon in the clearing in Toni Morrison's *Beloved* is an example of life sustaining worship:

> Baby Suggs called the women to her. "Cry," she told them. "For the living and the dead. Just cry." And without covering their eyes the women let loose. It started that way: laughing children, dancing men, crying women and then it got mixed up. Women stopped crying and danced; men sat down and cried; children danced, women laughed, children cried until, exhausted and riven, all and each lay about the Clearing damp and gasping for breath.[28]

---

28. Morrison, *Beloved*, 88.

Part I

This type of worship is an exhortation to victorious self-love, communal affirmation, and the spirituality of personhood. She calls the children to laugh, the men to dance and the women to cry, to mourn the living and the dead. Then she calls them to love themselves—all the parts of themselves:

> In the silence that followed, Baby Suggs, holy, offered up to them her great big heart. . . ."Here," she said, "in this here place, we flesh; flesh that weeps, laughs; flesh that dances on bare feet in grass. Love it. Love it hard. Yonder they do not love your flesh. They despise it. . . . No more do they love the skin on your back. Yonder they flay it. And O my people they do not love your hands. Those they only use, tie, bind, chop off and leave empty. Love your hands! Love them! Raise them up and kiss them. Touch others with them, pat them together, stroke them on your face 'cause they don't love that either. You got to love it, you! And no, they ain't in love with your mouth. Yonder, out there, they will see it broken and break it again. What you say out of it they will not heed. . . .What you put into it to nourish your body they will snatch away and give leavins instead. No, they don't love your mouth. You got to love it.[29]

Shame, humiliation, anger, fear, and helplessness stifle mourning. Silence is an intimidating deterrent to mourning. When trauma is forced to go underground, it becomes suppressed, uncontrolled, and inherently unconscious. Baby Suggs invites her people to acknowledge their pain, their suffering, their trauma, their loss. When they have exhausted their tears, when the bodies have released the trauma through dancing, when they have healed their body and spirits with laughter, she instructs them to love themselves, every part of themselves because if they don't love themselves, they cannot love each other. Slave religion was a massive theological reinvention and a survival theology for a destroyed society. Spirituality and religion connect with the internal and the unconscious. As seen in the strong presence in the Armenian and Jewish populations and the diminished presence in the Native American population, religion and spirituality play an important part in maintaining community, identity, and culture.

---

29. Ibid., 88.

Chapter 4

Theological Review

Matthew V. Johnson, Flora Keshgegian, Shelly Rambo, Dominic Robinson

FOUR THEOLOGIANS HAVE BEEN instrumental in shaping this project. Dominic Robinson, Matthew V. Johnson, Shelly Rambo and Flora Keshgegian represent four different Christian traditions and cultural heritages, but they speak about the value of human dignity, experiencing God, mourning losses, and living with the trauma. Instead of an abstract discussion of the authors, I found it most helpful to talk about their work in the form of a literary review.

DOMINIC ROBINSON

Born in Lancaster, England in 1967, Dominic Robinson entered the Society of Jesus in 1991, and was ordained a Jesuit priest in 2002. He studied theology at St. Mary's College, University of St. Andrews; Heythrop College, University of London; Weston Jesuit School of Theology, Cambridge, Massachusetts, and researched his doctorate at the Pontifical Gregorian University, Rome. He has also studied philosophy, politics, and economics at Campion Hall, Oxford. He is currently Lecturer in Dogmatic Theology at Heythrop College, University of London, and works in adult religious education in the Archdiocese of Westminster.

Dominic Robinson in *Understanding The "Imago Dei": The Thought of Barth, von Balthasar and Moltmann*, examines the "*imago Dei*," human beings in the image of God, in conversation with three twentieth-century theologians: Karl Barth and Jürgen Moltmann from the Reformed Tradition, and Hans Urs von Balthasar, a Catholic theologian. He selected these three because each theologian, in his own tradition, advocates a reaffirmation of the doctrine of "*imago Dei.*" Robinson detects an "ecumenical movement" in the writing of Barth, Moltmann and von Balthasar, and all three return to similar sources in the Patristic, Medieval and Reformed traditions to develop their doctrines. The ecumenical bridge Robinson attempts to build is across aspects he describes as the "descendant"—that which stresses God's descending to earth in Christ, and the "ascendant"—that which focuses on the human person's orientation towards God.[1]

Through historical, analytical, and critical research, Robinson identifies a way to present an ecumenically-inspired Christocentric understanding of the "*imago Dei.*" He believes that the new interest in this doctrine among Christian authors of different traditions is an indication that theology is trying to say something about human dignity in the twenty-first century.

> There is a new recognition of the power here to show how it is in Christ that human beings find their sense of true value and their infinite horizon in a divine calling and destiny. The doctrine underlines Christ's presence in the world shining through all of humanity. This affects how theology speaks of contemporary concerns as it underscores our understanding of our responsibility for others graced with the same dignity, our care for the world around us and so of the ethical values which form a Christian conscience.[2]

In the first chapter, Robinson does an extensive biblical-historical-theological analysis of the sources used by all three theologians, and then dedicates a chapter to each. He introduces their life and times, their theological perspectives and then outlines their perspectives on the doctrine of "*imago Dei.*" Robinson's conclusion is:

> [T]hey all represent the importance of grounding the doctrine in Christ and his action in our lives. They all start their doctrine from above, not from below. The human being's creation in God's image is a theological topic which must be firmly rooted in the light of the truth about God, and in particular, his descent to us in Christ.

---

1. Robinson, *Understanding the "Imago Dei,"* 1.
2. Ibid., 4.

Only then can we explore the human condition from the perspective of its own ascent, desire and quest for God.[3]

Also in conversation with these theologians, Robinson engages Pope John Paul II and Pope Benedict XVI. Pope John Paul in his Encyclical, *Redemptor Hominis,* called on Christians to examine their collective consciences as to how they uphold and respect the dignity of the human person, particularly in the face of new threats to its fundamental place in morality, law, and political ideology. This call was rooted in the belief in the human being's new creation in Christ as his image on earth and in a vision of his supernatural calling.[4] Pope Benedict in his Encyclical, *Deus Caritas Est*, and building on the teaching of Pope Paul writes: "Being Christian is not the result of an ethical choice or a lofty idea, but the encounter with an event, a person, who gives life a new horizon and a new decisive direction."[5]

Robinson argues the need for the doctrine of *"imago Dei"* to be expanded to include the human response to God's creating us in God's image. It requires us to speak of our ongoing relationship with Christ which propels us outwards toward others, the human search for meaning, fulfillment, and destiny, and how we live out our calling to be God's image on earth in our relationship with others with whom we share a like dignity. It is important to account our ascent, our call to transcendence, of our ongoing friendship with God and with each other.

Robinson concludes that even though Barth reorients the doctrine in God, the element of human response is underdeveloped. And, in his final analysis of Moltmann, he does not think that Moltmann is anchored sufficiently in the centrality of Christ as the perfect image of God. Robinson's view is that Balthasar is the one theologian who developed the "ascent" most clearly and that these strengths are seen in comparison to Barth.

In his concluding reflections, Robinson writes that Balthasar enables the Christian community to speak more powerfully of human dignity and vocation. Human dignity is clearly God's presence within us which advances our ability to go beyond ourselves and develop a stronger relationship with God and with each other. "The human being, by virtue of Christ, possess a divinely-bestowed dignity, which at the same time calls him [or her]

---

3. Ibid., 27.
4. Ibid., 2.
5. Ibid., 3.

Part I

forward to play his [or her] part on Christ's mission and in his [or her] own spiritual pilgrimage."[6]

Robinson summarizes his work with the following statement: "To be created in the "*imago Dei*" means above all that we are loved infinitely by Christ who draws us into a life of love ultimately fulfilled in our divine destiny. It is the presence of Jesus Christ in each human being which gives him [her] his [her] special dignity as created in the "*imago Dei*."[7]

The enslaved African Americans recognized the presence of Jesus Christ and understood deeply what it meant to be made in the image of God, to embody that special dignity. The enslaved African Americans were convinced, as Pope Benedict stated, that being Christian was the result of an encounter with the person of Jesus Christ, who gave their life a new horizon beyond their enslaved existence and gave them a new decisive direction which was to be free.[8] For Pope Benedict,

> the passionate nature of the love of God in Jesus Christ for us gives us a sense of our special dignity as beloved and enkindles the desire to show this love to others. Saint John's Gospel describes that event in these words. "God so loved the world that he gave his only Son, that whoever believes in him should have eternal life." ... Since God has first loved us (Jn 4:10), love is now no longer a mere command, it is a response to the gift of love with which God draws near to us. ... It is from our encounter with him that we may understand more fully our own Christian identity and responsibility.[9]

Pope John Paul II constantly underlined that at the center of the Christian message was the dignity of the human person as one in whom Christ resides. He believed that Jesus Christ defines the Church's understanding of the human person's responsibilities as a moral agent which centers on Christ and the recognition of human dignity which flows from this.[10]

In agreement with the statement "to be created in the "*imago Dei*" is to be loved infinitely by Christ," the question is how does an enslaved person interpret "who draws us into a life of love ultimately fulfilled in our divine destiny?" In the context of chattel slavery, what is a life of love? What is the

6. Ibid., 160.
7. Ibid., 161.
8. Carter, *Prayer Tradition*, 47.
9. Robinson, *Understanding the "Imago Dei*," 168–69.
10. Ibid., 168.

divine destiny? What is God calling enslaved people to be and do while living in chattel slavery?

In her book, *Their Eyes Were Watching God*, Zora Neale Hurston depicts being created in the image of God in her description of Janie, the protagonist, who is seeking to be her authentic self.

> When God had made The Man [and Woman], God made them out of stuff that sung all the time and glittered all over. Then after that, some angels got jealous and chopped them into millions of pieces, but still they glittered and hummed. So those angels beat them down to nothing but sparks, but each little spark had a shine and a song. So they covered each one over with mud. And the lonesomeness in the sparks made them hunt for one another, but the mud is deaf and dumb. Like all the other tumbling mud-balls, Janie had tried to show her shine.[11]

For the enslaved African Americans, their vocation was to hunt for each other and show their shine; saving family and saving self.[12] They grabbed hold of God's message of love and they identified with Christ's suffering. Their "divine destiny" was survival and liberation. The enslaved African Americans recognized the value of each other and they recognized that God valued them. They believed they were made in God's image, and they were children of God, and God loved them.[13] For them the vocation was to live and sustain family and community in spite of the cruel oppression they were living under.

MATTHEW V. JOHNSON

Matthew Johnson gives insight into "*imago Dei*" as appropriated by an enslaved people. Johnson, a graduate of Morehouse College, earned his Master's and Doctor of Philosophy degrees in Philosophical Theology from the University of Chicago. He also completed two years of post-doctorate work in psychoanalytic training at Duke University in conjunction with the University of North Carolina at Chapel Hill. Dr. Johnson has a served on the faculty of Interdenominational Theological Center, Atlanta, GA and United Theological Seminary of the Twin Cities, Minneapolis, MN. Dr.

---

11. Hurston, *Their Eyes Were Watching God*, 86.
12. Berlin, *Many Thousands Gone*, 130; Raboteau, *Slave Religion*, 304–5.
13. Cooper-Lewter and Mitchell, *Soul Theology*, 112.

Part I

Johnson is the pastor of the Mt. Moriah Missionary Baptist Church Pratt City in Birmingham, Alabama.

Johnson is the author of three major theological works. *The Tragic Vision of African American Religion* (2010) is an analysis of African American religious subjectivity and understanding of the religious experience and its theological implications. *The Passion of the Lord: African American Reflections* (2005) is a book which presents the biblical, historical, and theological roots of African American views. *Onesimus Our Brother* (2012) examines the letter which contains so many of our unconscious assumptions about religion, race, and culture. His article, "The Middle Passage: Trauma and the Tragic Re-imagination of African American Theology" was accepted for publication in *The Journal of Pastoral Psychology*. As a novelist in the tone and tradition of Zora Neal Hurston, Johnson's first novel, *The Cicada's Song* (2006) adds to a rich treasure of African American literature. He is a member of the American Academy of Religion, and the International Society for Traumatic Stress Studies.

Growing up in the traditional African American Baptist tradition, Johnson began his ministry at the age of seventeen. He acknowledges that all parts of his life are filtered through his faith, including all its strengths and weaknesses, failures and fragmentations. Johnson believes that the most important contribution the African American culture can give to this world is its example of the strength of the human spirit at life's extremities.

Struggling with the problem of excessive suffering and evil, Johnson's key query in *The Tragic Vision of African American Religion* is: "What is the relation of God to human anguish? . . . What kind of God, or vision of ultimate reality, does the nature of human experience, suffering, and the religious response to it imply?"[14]

Johnson noticed a footnote in Cornel West's *Prophesy Deliverance* that referred to the African American experience as a sort of tragic Good Friday state of existence. This influenced Johnson's interest in the concepts of mourning, loss, longing, and desire in the African American religious experience. He writes,

> This book, then, is an examination of African Americans' experience of the Christian faith as they struggled to manufacture meaning out of the raw material of their pain and what their experience may suggest about the nature of ultimate reality as conceived within the framework of a transfigured Christian faith.

14. Johnson, *The Tragic Vision*, 2.

> It is my position that Africans and their biological, and no less spiritual and cultural progeny in the New World, African Americans, effectuated nothing less than a spiritual transvaluation of the Christian faith they were introduced to in the New World. This occurred as they availed themselves to the faith in the context of the marginalized existence. This "state of being" entailed, among other things, a distinctive mass experience of loss and longing, of marginalization, chronic mourning and pain. All of this was constitutive of a traumatic field that provided the existential context for the emergence of African American religious experience. African Americans found a powerful tool of expression, as well as a tool of spiritual and cultural adaptation, in the resources of a biblical faith.[15]

Johnson describes through process theology, Greek tragedy and psychoanalysis, an operational theology that kept the enslaved people alive. He proposes that African Americans transvalued Christianity as a byproduct of their ability to fashion a theology that gave them hope in the middle of great suffering.

> The key elements of the African American experience are chronic mourning and irretrievable loss. The Christian Gospel provided a response for the expression of the bittersweet tragic soul. The African American enslaved people created a transvalued Christian Gospel shaped by biblical themes and figures and their experience as chattel slavery. This transvalued Gospel facilitated life and ambiguity, fragmentation and pain while embracing its terrible truths without lapsing into denial. This tension created a space for both hope and sanity.[16]

Johnson describes two examples of the resilience of their human spirit. The first is his description of the "shout" as the authentic encounter of the human spirit facing the abyss, the horror, the state of nonbeing, in defiance. Shouting at death is a declaration of "I AM." It was the enslaved persons' refusal to allow themselves, whom they knew and believed to be created in the "*imago Dei*," to be destroyed. By this I mean that when enslaved persons yelled, called out, bawled, shrieked, bellowed, and screamed, they proclaimed, announced, and asserted their existence from the core of their being.

> In the belly of those floating whales [slave ships], consumed by the cruel greed of an insatiable appetite for profit, the African captive

15. Ibid., 4.
16. Ibid., 89.

groaned and regurgitated. He moaned and groaned until he found the melody that mirrored his wretchedness, and in expressing it thusly preserved and secured the value of his pain. In that magic moment of ghastly horror and naked heroism, a new spirituality was born.[17]

The other example of resistance is the seminal trait and strongest recognizable component of the African American experience, the permeating sense of anguish and sorrow. The suffering of the enslaved African Americans is the essential foundation of their religion. It is the underlying structure on which their songs and sermons were created. The collective experience of generations of loss, longing, suffering, and sorrow are African American worship and song which Johnson describes as follows:

> Traditional African American religious expression and spirituality in its most authentic mode approaches the character of a dirge or lament. . . . There is a powerful strain of something approaching joy present in the mix, but it is wrapped in a foil of sorrow, anguish and lament. . . . The joy of African American religious experience is a joy dogged by reality, it was an affirmation and a longing. Sorrow for the circumstances they were in and longing for change and ultimate justice. Affirmation of the worthwhileness of life in the face of the threat of meaninglessness and nonbeing.[18]

For Johnson, it is the experience of God that is central to African American religion and culture, and the greatest outcome of that interaction of African Americans' Christian faith is strength. Engagement with the divine was, and is, the source of strength. God is real, tangible, and identifiable, and makes the believer "feel like going on."

> At the existential level . . . the primary existential reality for the African American is strength and more to the point, God's strength. This plays itself out in God's ability to share their burden and His strength and as a direct result, their capacity to successfully undergo frightening, potentially ruinous experiences. God's goodness is conceived of in terms of His "willingness" to do the same. . . . The strength to go on remains and flourishes in the face of unanswered questions and in the presence of deep and abiding suffering. . . . Strength commands in its wake the traits of endurance, commitment, and perseverance, as well as the images of toil, labor and lifting. It is the yield of the dynamic engagement of life at its fullest.

17. Ibid., 95.
18. Ibid., 90.

> Strength is the complement of the depth affirmation of being, of life. In a word, strength is the result of living; it is the substance of life, it is the measure of being.[19]

Johnson is of the opinion that if Christianity is to continue to be considered a viable religion in today's cultural environment of mass shootings, war, gang violence, financial instability, and natural disasters, serious attention needs to be given to African American religious consciousness. The world would greatly benefit from understanding African American religious consciousness because it demonstrates how the human spirit can survive extreme, chronic, abusive suffering.

Johnson's historical and theological assessment of the African American contribution to Christianity gives encouragement and hope to people who are suffering from trauma, oppression, and injustice. It offers a model of worship and biblical interpretation that provides hope and strength. African American worship is a tenacious rejoicing because at its core is a proclamation of innermost yearning. The African American community has inherited a tremendous gift from its ancestors to equip them to sustain its faith and confidence in the face of adversity which is a part of life. When African Americans talk about the nature of God and religious beliefs related to the Holy Spirit, it is a strengthening force that is constantly present during times of fragmentations, fractures and schisms. Johnson's phrase "practicing theology in an African American key" is a challenge to other theologians to reconsider some central issues of the faith. It provides the strength and hope to endure chronic pervasive suffering. African American religious consciousness can provide strength to people at life's extremities.

SHELLY RAMBO

Shelly Rambo is a theologian who has taken up the challenge to reconsider central issues of the Christian faith. She is a constructive theologian, who engages the textual tradition of Christianity with particular attention to postmodern literary criticism and analysis. Trained as both a systematic and constructive theologian, she is interested in how classical themes in the Christian tradition interact with and inform contemporary discourses around suffering, trauma, and violence. Her book, *Spirit and Trauma: A Theology of Remaining*, forges a theology of the Spirit through engagements

---

19. Ibid., 125–26.

PART I

with postmodern biblical hermeneutics, a theology of Holy Saturday, and contemporary trauma theory. Her current research explores the significance of resurrection wounds in the Christian tradition in connection to contemporary discourses about wounding, both in popular culture and in the study of trauma. Her teaching and research interests include: feminist theory and theology, postmodern theology, pneumatology, and trauma studies. Through a series of faculty grants funded by the Center for Practical Theology and the Lilly Endowment, she has developed and presented workshops that offer religious leaders critical tools for thinking theologically about trauma. She received her Doctor of Philosophy in theology from Emory University's Graduate Division of Religion in 2004, a Master of Divinity from Princeton Theological Seminary and Sacred Theology Masters from Yale Divinity School.

Rambo's initial study of trauma began while at Yale University in the 1990s, where researchers were studying the effect of the Holocaust on survivors.[20] Her education was expanded through conversations with military chaplains, survivors of sexual abuse, community leaders working in post disaster areas, and urban leaders wrestling with the realities of immigration enforcement and street violence.[21] Witnessing the impact of trauma on individuals and communities, she began to rethink the claims of Christian faith. Rambo studies trauma because it poses the most challenges to persons of faith—the question of suffering. She focuses on answering the big questions: Where is God in the suffering? Who are we to be as people of faith in response to suffering and the suffering around us?[22]

Rambo recounts the words of Julius Lee at a Churches Supporting Churches meeting in New Orleans two years after Katrina. Deacon Lee, a retired member of the Unites States Air Force and deacon of Greater St. Luke Baptist Church, protested the fact that Hurricane Katrina was not simply a singular event that took place in August 2005. It was an event that continues, that persists in the present. Deacon Lee told those in attendance, "Things are not back to normal. People keep telling us to get over it already. The storm is gone, but the 'after the storm' is always here . . ."[23]

In her book, Rambo defines trauma as the suffering that does not go away. "It persists in symptoms that live on in the body, in the intrusive

20. Rambo, "Shelly Rambo."
21. Rambo, *Spirit and Trauma*, xiv.
22. Rambo, "Shelly Rambo."
23. Rambo, *Spirit and Trauma*, 1.

fragments of memories that return. It persists in symptoms that live on in communities, in the layers of past violence that constitute present ways of relating.... Life after the storm, people in New Orleans can tell you, is not life as they once knew it. It is life continually marked by the ongoingness of death."[24]

Rambo's main argument is that trauma blurs the line between life and death, that the aftereffects of the traumatic event linger, and one must learn to live in the lingering. Trauma is the unintegrated experience. It is the overwhelming force of the event. The human emotional and physical systems shut down. Often the ability to speak about it is lost. Life becomes reorganized around the trauma. Unintegrated trauma can be re-triggered, and a person can relive the event as if it were just happening. It is called "traumatic haunting." She understands that ability to live in the lingering as witnessing.

Rambo gives an explanation of how the symbolic meanings of Holy Saturday can help trauma survivors become witnesses. Holy Saturday, the day of the Holy Week between Good Friday and Easter Sunday, symbolizes the time between the cross and the resurrection, death and life. She believes most Christians ignore Holy Saturday and move too quickly from Good Friday to Easter Sunday. She contends most of us, and especially trauma survivors, do not live a Good Friday or Easter Sunday life, but live somewhere in the middle, living a Holy Saturday life with its remnants of the big and little traumas of life.

Rambo draws on the theologies of Hans Urs von Balthasar, Adrienne von Speyr and readings of the Johannine gospel to articulate her vision of the middle territory. Through Balthasar's and Speyr's work, she explores Holy Saturday, that middle day located between Good Friday's crucifixion and Easter Sunday's resurrection. In her reading of the Johannine gospel she examines the "witness of the middle movements of the disciples between cross and resurrection."[25] Rambo then presents her theology of the Spirit. She challenges common theological conceptions of Spirit as solely a forward moving life force. Instead, she argues that when seen through the lens of trauma, Spirit is better conceived of as a sustaining force that dwells in the middle territory, or in what remains following a traumatic experience. Rambo writes: "But a theology of the Spirit, as I develop it here, is less clearly the life principle and more a sustaining power that continually

---

24. Ibid., 2.
25. Ibid., 11.

PART I

witnesses the ruptures, moving between death and life."[26] Finally, Rambo asks readers to imagine what it would mean to think about this type of witness—the witness of the middle territory of trauma—as redemptive.[27] She believes that the middle speaks to the perplexing space of survival. The middle, she claims, is a largely untheologized site, because the middle is overshadowed by Good Friday and Easter Sunday.

Rambo identifies a theological perspective that the enslaved African Americans developed in response to the 246 years (approximately eight generations) of intense, massive and chronic trauma of chattel slavery. The sustaining force she names the "Middle Spirit" is the same sustaining force of the Holy Spirit; the love of Jesus; and the righteous power of God that gave the enslaved people the resiliency to endure the persistent peril and chronic trauma of chattel slavery. Rambo offers a contemporary theological perspective within the context of trauma that also recognizes the unspeakable trauma of grief, loss, and abuse the survivors and descendants of chattel slavery carry in their minds, bodies, and spirits, as well as survivors who carry the trauma of natural disasters like Katrina and Super Storm Sandy; gun violence like Columbine, Virginia Tech, Sandy Hook, Baltimore, Charleston, Paris, and San Bernardino; terrorism like 9/11; war; poverty; gang violence; sexual and physical abuse. She gives hope to those who feel abandoned by their suffering. Life will never be the same, but life is still possible living in the middle of the lingering residue.

FLORA KESHGEGIAN

Living in the "middle of the residue" is the quest that prompted Flora Keshgegian to find a way that allows one to move forward, respecting the systematic past, honoring the ancestors. Flora Keshgegian is a seminary professor, Episcopal priest, and a theologian who applies trauma theory to Christian theology. Her writing draws on her experiences growing up in an immigrant home and as a child of survivors of the Armenian Genocide. She is particularly interested in what it means to live an abundant life, especially with a legacy of trauma and suffering. She also explores the nature and dynamics of power, particularly given cultural and gender differences.

Keshgegian attended public schools in Philadelphia and the University of Pennsylvania, where she earned a Bachelor of Arts degree in Religious

---

26. Ibid., 12.
27. Schumm, "A Review of Spirit and Trauma," 15, 334–35.

Thought. In addition, she has a Master of Divinity degree from the Philadelphia Divinity School and a Doctor of Philosophy degree from the joint doctoral program of Boston College and Andover Newton Theological School. Currently, she is associate professor of Pastoral Theology and Women in Ministry at the Church Divinity School of the Pacific in Berkeley, California. Previously, she served as associate chaplain (1984–1998) and as faculty ombudsperson (2006–2009) at Brown University.

Keshgegian began this research because she felt burdened by the memories of the Armenian Genocide that were continually reinforced by her parents, church, and Armenian community. The victims of the genocide are portrayed as martyrs who died for their faith and their ethnic identity. To forget was seen as a betrayal that dishonored and dismissed their sacrifice. The struggle for Keshgegian was how to honor her history without being stuck in a victimized way of seeing the world. She did not want to discount the suffering and forget it, but she did not want it to consume her and keep her from moving forward and living life to the fullest.

Redeeming Memories: A Theology of Healing and Transformation describes her experiences both as the child of survivors of the Armenian Genocide and as a college chaplain ministering to women who had suffered childhood sexual abuse. The book is an outgrowth of her dissertation "To Know By Heart: Toward a Theology of Remembering for Salvation," portions of which have been included.

The purpose of this book is to remember, from the perspectives of those who have been victimized, in such a way that we might "re-member" Christianity and society. Her approach is best defined as a Christian feminist, political theologian, and she identifies herself as a "white, privileged, ethnic minority woman."[28]

Keshgegian looks at several groups who have been victimized and abused: sexually abused women, the Armenian and Jewish communities who experienced genocide, African Americans, and women. Against these populations, she investigates how Christianity has played a part in the domination and oppression of these groups. Keshgegian cautions the reader on the complexity of remembering.

> People who have been marginalized in society and whose voices have been suppressed are seeking to uncover their pasts in order to claim the present in a different way, and to change the future. They are, in a sense, on a quest for identity and recognition, to

---

28. Keshgegian, *Redeeming Memories*, 11.

> know themselves and place themselves differently in the world. At the heart of these quests is a desire for empowerment, to claim and exercise power in their own lives and in the world.[29]

Remembering for Keshgegian is to listen to the silenced stories of the oppressed and Christianity's participation in the silencing. To be redeemed, one must first be heard. Asking the question "what is to be remembered and for what reason?" she offers four motivations for remembering: 1) to indict the dominant culture for harm it has perpetuated, 2) to transform the suffering or claim a past that is more than victimization, 3) to look for resources in the past in order to confirm present directions or bolster present agendas of identity, and 4) to emphasize empowerment in the present that will lead to a quest for stories of agency.[30] She concludes that, in spite of all the conflict and complexity of motives, the fundamental motivation is to transcend the pain, loss and trauma, and enable life and hope.

To promote the movement toward life and hope, Keshgegian identifies three distinctive types of remembrance: 1) of suffering and loss, 2) of resistance and agency, and 3) of connection with life and wholeness not defined by the suffering.

> Suffering and loss must be remembered and mourned... Although the loss is never forgotten or restored, grieving and mourning eventually allow the pain and losses to be less dominant.... Being able to name and claim what people did to survive, even in seemingly impossible situations, is vitally important to their own process of healing and transformation and to the process of witnessing.... Remembering resistance enables resilience, the ability of human beings to go on living.... Ultimately, the purpose of remembering and of witness is to expand the narrative for living for those who survive and their heirs and for the sake of human flourishing and life abundant beyond surviving.... Such remembrance entails making connections between the particularities of the experience of victimization and other experiences, between oneself or one's group and others.[31]

Keshgegian then turns her attention to the church for ways it can be a community of remembrance and witness. She writes:

---

29. Ibid., 90.
30. Ibid., 112.
31. Ibid., 122.

> The purpose of the church is to remember God and God's action especially in Jesus Christ. . . . Remembering confers identity. . . . Our memories do not only shape who we are—there is a way in which we have no identity if we have no memory. . . . The church not only needs to remember, but what and how it remembers will affect its nature and mission. The church's defining memory is the narrative of who we are in relationship to God in Jesus Christ. Christian identity is shaped in relation to that narrative.[32]

As a clergywoman in a sacramental tradition that places importance on the Eucharist and the body of the suffering servant, Keshgegian expands the meaning of this ritual by suggesting that the emphasis not be just on Jesus' crucifixion and death, but also on his life and resurrection. She says the resurrection is not about Jesus breaking the bonds of sin and death, or God the almighty doing battle on behalf of humanity, but the resurrection is about the power of life to persist and prevail. It is not about the survival of the individual but about the continuation of life itself. It can and should be both the memorial meal remembering a traumatic event of suffering, degradation, and death, giving those who are oppressed and abused an opportunity to bring their suffering and pain to this table knowing that God understands and is with them in their suffering. But it should also bring to memory Jesus' life and resurrection. Commanded to continue to enact this ritual until Jesus returns, implies an end to the way things are and a new and better way of life. That implication facilitates hope.

Keshgegian develops a model of church whose work is to be redemptive and transformative, shaped by the story of the life, ministry, death, and resurrection of Jesus Christ. "The church as a community of remembrance honors and preserves memories of suffering; evokes, recognizes and validates memories of resistance and agency; and actively supports, embodies, and celebrates memories of connections and life affirmation."[33] She suggests rituals of healing to recognize the woundedness and to celebrate the resilience and spirit of those who survived. This can be done in worship and ritual, preaching and teaching, and social and political action. What she suggests is what would be healing in the African American church community: mourning the history of chattel slavery and the effects of transgenerational trauma, honoring the resistance and resilience of the ancestors in order to renew hope, and celebrating life for those living and

---

32. Ibid., 202.
33. Ibid., 211.

Part I

for future generations within the context of the African American church community.

SUMMARY

Robinson encapsulates his work with the following statement: "To be created in the "*imago Dei*" means above all that we are loved infinitely by Christ who draws us into a life of love ultimately fulfilled in our divine destiny. It is the presence of Jesus Christ in each human being which gives him his special dignity as created in the "*imago Dei*."[34]

Johnson gives an example of the manifestation of the "*imago Dei*" in his description of the "shout" as the authentic encounter of the human spirit facing the abyss, the horror, the state of nonbeing, in defiance. Shouting at death is a declaration of "I AM." It was the enslaved people's refusal to allow themselves, whom they knew and believed to be created in the "*imago Dei*," to be destroyed.

Rambo asks readers to imagine what it would mean to be the witness of the middle territory of trauma. She believes that the middle speaks to the perplexing space of survival. The middle, she claims, is a largely untheologized site, because the middle is overshadowed by Good Friday and Easter Sunday. The middle territory she refers to has been and continues to be the only theologized site from which life has been sustained for the enslaved Africans and African Americans. However, Holy Saturday should have a prominent position in the liturgical calendar. Before the resurrection story, there needs to be a clearer expression of the "middle" or the "tragic vision," an acknowledgement of living with the residue of trauma, and a recognition that there is sustenance to continue living, even if it is not the triumphant victorious, problem free, worry free existence that is so commonly associated with the resurrection story.

As Keshgegian recommends, the communion table can and should be the memorial meal remembering a traumatic event of suffering, degradation, and death. It gives those who are oppressed and abused an opportunity to bring their suffering and pain to this table knowing that God understands and is with them in their suffering. The church should also bring to memory Jesus' life and resurrection and continue to enact this ritual until Jesus returns. Doing so implies an end to the way things are and a new and better way of life. That implication is a catalyst for hope.

34. Ibid., 161.

Chapter 5

Course Description
Roots Matter: Healing History, Honoring Heritage, Renewing Hope

THE PROJECT SEGMENT OF the Doctor of Ministry requirements was a six week-class. The class was an exploratory exercise in developing a method to attend to the transgenerational trauma of the transatlantic and domestic slave trade within the context of the African American church community in Virginia. The goal of the class was for participants to: 1) become knowledgeable of trauma and transgenerational trauma literature; 2) become familiar with the history of the transatlantic and domestic slave trade through the lens of trauma; 3) identify biblical themes and theological concepts of trauma, suffering, forgiveness and healing; 4) create a genogram using either a stencil template or genogram software of at least three generations of family members; 5) design individually and collectively healing rituals and prayers; 6) participate in a closing generational healing service. Six two-hour classes were held on the campus of Union Presbyterian Seminary.

A letter of invitation was sent to the twenty prospective participants three months before the class was to begin. The letter explained the purpose of the class and that it was a pilot offered to partially fulfill the requirements for a Doctor of Ministry degree. The dates, time, and place were given to the prospective participants, as were the class objectives and requirements. Because of the emotional nature of the material, and for the well-being of the participants, the students were urged to commit to attend all classes.

To remove as many barriers as possible, the class was offered at no cost and food was provided thirty minutes before the class formally started.

Part I

Childcare was also available. The invitees had seven days to reply. Those who did not reply within the time frame were contacted again via email. When all responses were received (sixteen), a confirmation email was sent notifying them that they would be contacted a few weeks before class was to start.

Two weeks before the class started, an email was sent with instructions on how to prepare for the first class. First, they were asked to find a prayer partner, someone to talk with and pray with during the six weeks of class. Second, they were asked to gather family stories, and were given a website link to assist them with ways to ask questions in interviews with family members. Finally, they were asked to confirm that they were still going to be able to participate. Four of the sixteen responded that they would not be able to participate.

Following is the general class outline. The intent was to incorporate multiple activities to accommodate different adult learning styles.

Class Outline

6:00 p.m.	Food and fellowship
6:30 p.m.	Opening prayer and video clip
6:40 p.m.	Cinquain devotional exercise
6:50 p.m.	Genogram process check-in
7:00 p.m.	Conversation about previous week's article or class questions
7:15 p.m.	Offerings (items relating to the subjects discussed that are personally significant to the participant)
7:30 p.m.	Break
7:40 p.m.	Introduction of topic of the week
8:00 p.m.	Freewriting exercise
8:15 p.m.	Distribution of article and questions for next week
8:20 p.m.	Closing prayer

Class Topics

1.1 Orientation, The Genogram and Family Systems

1.2 Old Testament Family Stories

1.3 Guest Speakers' Personal Testimony *and* Generational Trauma in Jewish, Native American and Armenian History

1.4 Generational Trauma in African American History

1.5 The African American Religious Tradition of Resiliency and Hope

1.6 Generational Healing Communion Ceremony

CLASS 1: ORIENTATION, THE GENOGRAM, AND FAMILY SYSTEMS

Class objectives: 1) to introduce the class structure, 2) to establish participant expectations, and 3) to explain participant responsibilities.

After the welcome, opening prayer, reading from *Prayers for Dark People* by W. E. B. Dubois[1] and housekeeping announcements, there was a review of the purpose of the class. Following the class introduction exercise, notebooks were distributed which contained a consent form (appendix A), syllabus (appendix B), instructions on how to write a cinquain, how to freewrite, and examples of offerings for the healing service. The consent form was read out loud and any questions about it answered. It was signed with classmates as witnesses and turned in. The syllabus was reviewed and questions about the exercises were answered.

After a ten-minute break, the homework activity, which had been sent out in an email two weeks before, was reviewed. The assignment was to be prepared to share family stories. The introduction to the genogram and family systems followed. The workbook, *A Family Genogram Workbook*, by Israel Galindo,[2] and a geometric template were distributed to the class. Because creating a genogram is time and labor intensive, placing this topic in the first class allowed the maximum amount of time for the participants to gather and record family information.

Next, new homework assignments were given. Participants were asked to freewrite about the experience of the class, to begin work on their family genograms, and to read the article distributed, "Genogram and African American Families: Employing Family Strengths of Spirituality, Religion, and Extended Family Network" by Annie McCullough Chavis.[3]

The class was closed in prayer.

---

1. Dubois, *Prayers for Dark People*.
2. Galindo, *A Family Genogram Workbook*.
3. Chavis. "Genograms and African American Families," 30–36.

Part I

CLASS 2: OLD TESTAMENT FAMILY STORIES

Class objectives: 1) to identify in scripture references to generational blessings and curses, and 2) to illustrate positive and negative traits of biblical families.

As part of the devotional exercise and after the opening prayer, the class watched a video clip from *Africans in America: American's Journey through Slavery*.[4] The class then wrote and read their cinquain, a five-lined, diamond-shaped poem which incorporates verbal, analytical, reading and writing skills. Following the devotional, there was a check-in on the progress of their genograms and time for questions. There was discussion of the assignment article and participants turned in their free writing of the article. After the break, each participant presented the weekly offering, an item that was related to the topic or subject and was personally significant to him or her. Items included, but were not limited, to prayers, music, photographs, art, books and household items.

To introduce the topic of the week, a genogram of the three generations of Abraham was presented from a family systems perspective. Using a biblical story in this way provided an example of how to recognize generational patterns of behaviors and events in the genogram form. A summary of the presented material was distributed with the reading assignment of a book review of *The Body Remembers* by Babette Rothschild.[5]

The class ended with a closing prayer.

CLASS 3: GENERATIONAL TRAUMA IN JEWISH, ARMENIAN, AND NATIVE AMERICAN HISTORY

Class objectives: 1) to introduce individuals who have participated in a generational healing prayer class and service, and 2) to present research information on trauma and generational trauma in other cultures.

After the opening prayer, the cinquain exercise was omitted in order to allow maximum time for the guest speakers. The first speaker was an Episcopal priest, a former staff member at Christian Healing Ministries in Jacksonville, Florida, the rector of an Episcopal church in Powhatan, Virginia and cofounder of a healing prayer ministry in Richmond, Virginia. The second speaker was a consultant coach whose expertise is in addiction

4. Fayer, *Africans In America*.
5. Rothschild., *Body Remembers*.

COURSE DESCRIPTION

recovery and traumatic brain injury. The executive director of a nonprofit recovery program in Williamsburg, Virginia, the second speaker participated in the healing prayer program led by the first speaker. The speakers told of their experiences and insights while working on their genograms and of the results of prayer for their families. A question and answer period followed. The class found their testimonies very helpful because it gave them an idea of what to look for and some of the possible outcomes when working with their own genograms. Because the first half of the class was set aside for the guest speakers, the participants were given a choice to give an update on their genogram progress, or to share their weekly offering, or to comment on the article given for homework.

Turning to the research done by Yael Danieli, Maria Yellow Horse Brave Heart, and Diane Kupelian, the second half of the class discussion was on the recognition and transmission of generational trauma presented in the articles. Two articles were distributed for the next weekly reading assignment: "Cutting Edge: Christian Imperialism and the Transatlantic Slave Trade" by Katie G. Cannon,[6] and "The African-American Experience: Forced Immigration and Transgenerational Trauma by Maurice Apprey.[7] The class ended with a closing prayer.

CLASS 4: GENERATIONAL TRAUMA IN AFRICAN AMERICAN HISTORY

Class objectives: 1) to identify trauma types and traumatic events in African American history, and 2) to compare similarities to and differences among Jewish, Armenian, and Native American transgenerational trauma.

A temporary classroom change and technical video difficulties did not allow the cinquain portion of the devotional exercise to be completed after the opening prayer. The class gave updates on their progress with the genogram and discussed the articles that had been assigned. The insights gleaned from the assigned readings and the material presented on the definition of 14 trauma types, the traumatic incidents of chattel slavery in African American history, and the resulting expressions of the trauma in the lives of the descendants were discussed during the first half of the class. After the break, the class shared their offerings. Research was presented and handouts were provided from the work of Elaine Pinderhughes,"The

---

6. Cannon, "Cutting Edge," 127–34.

7. Apprey, "The African-American Experience," 70–75.

PART I

Multigenerational Transmission of Loss and Trauma: The African American Experience,"[8] Joy DeGruy's *Post Traumatic Slave Syndrome*[9] and "The National Child Traumatic Stress Network" definitions of different trauma types (appendix C). To provide an emotional and psychological balance, the participants were reminded to identify resilience and resistance in the history and in their families. Two articles were assigned for the next week's reading, "The Middle Passage, Trauma and the Tragic Re-Imagination of African American Theology" by Matthew Johnson,[10] and "Racism and Economics: The Perspective of Oliver Cox" by Katie Geneva Cannon.[11] The class ended with closing prayer.

CLASS 5: THE AFRICAN AMERICAN RELIGIOUS TRADITION OF RESILIENCY AND HOPE

Class objective: to identify the strengths and resilience in the African American religious tradition.

After the opening prayer, the video segment for the cinquain devotional was from *Unchained Memories: Readings from the Slave Narratives*.[12] The narratives were about families, and how some were willing to endure beatings in order to see family members on other plantations. After a progress update on the genograms, the reflections on the reading material, and the sharing of the offerings, the topic for discussion became the material introduced on the resilience and resistance of African Americans, and how they were expressed in their theology and religious practices. Materials were distributed on the theological and spiritual impact of major trauma, and how mourning facilitates healing by creating an emotional and spiritual space for hope to exist.[13] In preparation for the last class, which was the healing service, the participants were asked to write a lament to express whatever loss or grief they had for themselves and for their families. They were also asked to write a list of all strengths and talents they recognized in their families and to list the pain, suffering, tragedy, grief, and loss to be of-

8. Pinderhughes, "The Multigenerational Transmission," 161–81.
9. DeGruy Leary, *Post Traumatic Slave Syndrome*.
10. Johnson,"Middle Passage," 541–61.
11. Cannon "Racism and Economics," 3–20.
12. Gates, *Unchained Memories*.
13. Carter, *Prayer Tradition*; Richo, *Five Things*; Janoff-Bulman, *Shattered Assumptions*.

fered in prayer. They were encouraged to bring items that were meaningful to share and reflect on during the service.

CLASS 6: GENERATIONAL HEALING COMMUNION CEREMONY

Class objectives: 1) to obtain feedback from participants about the effectiveness of the class, and 2) to offer opportunities for participants to pray for generational healing of their families. An evaluation form was sent to the participants to complete and bring to the last class. (See appendix D.) The first half of this last class was dedicated to evaluation and recommendations. A certificate of participation and a copy of an advertisement seeking capture of a runaway slave were given to each participant. Evaluations were turned in at the break.

The second half of the class was the healing service. The participants were given a program (appendix E) that was divided into three sections: Healing History: A time for lamentation and grieving for the family; Honoring Heritage: A time to celebrate the resilience and talents of the family; and Renewing Hope: A time for prayer for healing for themselves and their families. Each segment was introduced with meditative music and a reading. As each participant offered a lament or blessing or petition for prayer, the class would respond with an affirmation. The service then transitioned with music to a communion service, followed by a litany using Margaret Walker's poem *For My People,* and then benediction. The participants were reminded of the follow-up meeting to be held in February to share what, if anything, significant had happened that could be attributed to being part of the class.

Chapter 6

Conclusion

Findings, Recommendations, and Further Study

CLASS EVALUATIONS

Evaluations were emailed to the class participants a week before the last class. (See Appendix D.) They were asked to complete them and bring them to the last class. Additional copies were available for those who had not brought one with them. Ten evaluations were turned in. One participant was out of the country and did not attend the last class. One participant did not turn in any written assignments with exception of the consent form. The evaluation form was a combination of yes/no questions, rating scales, and open-ended questions designed to engender suggestions. The areas evaluated were: class expectations; clarity of presentations of materials by presenters; rating of facilities; and usefulness of materials.

Class composition—The class was half clergy and half non-clergy (excluding the leader).

Physical space—There was only one comment about having a larger classroom. The doors to the building were locked for security. The entry door was monitored, but on more than one occasion, a person had to call to be let in. Parking was well lighted with easy access.

Food and childcare—Providing food was greatly appreciated. It eliminated the necessity to stop for food on the way to class, and everyone had

CONCLUSION

time to make the transition from work to class. Childcare was used twice as emergency backup by two classmates on different occasions.

Length of class—The overall consensus was that the class was too short to cover all of the material. It was suggested that class time be increased to three hours to allow for breakout sessions. Also suggested was for class sessions to be lengthened to: eight weeks; twelve weeks; two days per month for ten months; a combination retreat and class format with an opening twenty-four hour retreat plus six two-hour weekly classes, with a closing twenty-four hour retreat; or a retreat format of nine twenty-four hour monthly retreats.

Reading assignments—The consensus was more time needed to be spent on the articles.

Writing assignments—One person did not turn in any written assignments, however that person did make important contributions to the class conversations. Only one participant turned in all the assignments. In reference to the freewrite exercise, a suggestion was made to make it an option for those who felt restricted by the time limit and wanted to write more.

Class activities—All learning styles were taken into consideration in presenting the material. There was a suggestion to assign videos to watch outside of class.

Genogram—The class wanted more hands-on instruction with the genogram, suggesting that their genograms be brought to class and more time spent on questions about them.

General content—There were suggestions for more information on the following:

- childhood trauma and how it affects adults
- Post Traumatic Stress Disorder
- stories of resilience, resistance, and redemption in African American history
- instruction and practice with healing prayer exercises
- coping mechanisms

Next steps—The participants wanted clearer suggestions about what to do after the class was finished. The class also wanted more information

Part I

on ways to integrate the lessons learned to help people move forward, e.g., what to do if you find yourself returning or refocusing on the same issues.

Recommended audiences—The class suggested that groups who could benefit from the experience include: seminary students who work in African American churches, African American church groups, pastoral care groups seeking an elective for credit or CEUs, Clinical Pastoral Education (CPE) students, and social science (social work, psychology) students. The course content could also be modified for secular settings including lifelong learning programs.

LEADER EVALUATION

In agreement with the participants the class could have easily been eight weeks instead of six. However, the final decision for six weeks was made for the following reasons: 1) to reduce the time commitment for volunteer participants, 2) to generate an achievable amount of new material, and 3) to allow sufficient time to complete the initial dissertation draft.

The class became so engaged with the material that by the third class, there was no time to review the handouts related to the new material for the week. For example, intercessory prayer was briefly discussed. It was anticipated to be a major point of discussion, but in retrospect, with this particular class, this was not a new topic. They were all familiar with the concept of intercessory prayer. There was more interest in pursuing subject matter that was new or unfamiliar. This was a positive dynamic; however it reinforces the need to lengthen the number of classes offered.

Anticipating painful and visceral reactions to the subject matter, I selected people for the class whom I knew and who were familiar with each other. All of them knew at least two others in the class. In doing so, the sense of safety and intimacy was enhanced. This was a highly educated group who said the material was complex and required more time to process and discuss. Using their reactions and feedback to the subject matter and materials, consideration will be made in selecting documents to use for future classes in other settings.

The stories they shared in the sessions reflected the similarities and differences. Five were natives of Virginia (two Richmond natives); four were from the North (Massachusetts, New Jersey, and Ohio [2]); two were

CONCLUSION

from the South (North Carolina, Georgia) and one was from the West (Texas). Their personal family stories ran the emotional gamut from speechless pain to laughing so hard that people were crying. It seemed as if the older participants grieved deeper and harder.

There were several surprises. The genogram became a three-generation project for one family. One participant wanted to know if work like this could be done in Haiti. Another participant saw a use with her patients in the hospital.

The offerings were very popular. All participants brought at least one item and shared the significance of what they brought. It was a way of learning about each other in a multifaceted, non-threatening way.

The homework freewrites were very helpful in designing the healing service, e.g., their writing about the music that was significant in their spiritual journey gave input into the selection of music for the service.

Designing a variety of teaching activities using all the senses fostered frequent personal engagement with the material. It gave the participants the opportunity to own the subject matter and use it in ways that were meaningful to them. This also decreased the necessity for long lectures.

This was an expensive class to offer. (See Table 1.) Careful considerations must be given to how to manage the cost to offer the program. And, finally, properly allocating sufficient time for learning activities, appropriately introducing new information and effectively leading class discussions are tasks that will improve with additional experience.

CLASS DISCOVERIES

The class participants were sent eight questions two weeks before the follow-up meeting which had been scheduled during the fifth class session and held four months after the last class. Only two completed the eight questions before the class, therefore three of the original questions were handed out at the follow-up class. All eleven of the twelve participants who were present responded to at least one of the three questions. Several themes emerged from the responses: 1) the "aha" moment, 2) changes in family relationships, 3) interest in family history, 4) church relationships, 5) personal changes in attitude and behavior, 6) understanding of generational trauma, 7) impact of the genogram, and 8) impact of the healing service.

The most heartfelt example of the "aha" moment was expressed by one of the male participants.

Part I

We were having a meeting of the minds about our assigned reading.... As I looked around the room and soaked in the words coming from each person, it became more and more evident that the only other voice in the room that sounded like mine was coming from the man sitting next to me. All of the other voices were the sweet, and usually confident voices of secure, opinionated, and educated women. But in this moment there was something else in their voices. There was a mixture of anxiety and subdued anger ... an underlying sense of frustration ... As I sat and listened to them, I realized that I was not as angry and anxious as they were. I was not feeling the same thing that they all, as a group, felt. I was void of understanding and separate from them. I wanted to know why. I questioned myself as to how I could not share any of the feelings that were being expressed in the room, especially since they were such intense emotions. It was at that point that I realized that it was because I was not a woman. My fears were not the same as theirs because what was being discussed was the victimization and rape of women. I had an intellectual understanding of the concept, but it came to a full realization while sitting in a room full of women who I had grown to respect and care for. In that moment, I understood and could feel (the ability to feel is the most important) several things that I was previously not in tune with: 1) I was not one of them and I had grown up in an environment that didn't foster that type of understanding of women. (There were three males and my mother in my immediate family and we were never consciously taught how to respect, understand, care for and empathize with women as individuals or communally.) 2) I realized that not understanding affected my ability to fully understand my role as a protector in a family and societal setting. 3) Because I was so painfully unaware of something that all of these women were aware of, it gave me a better understanding of how racism can persist. (That is to say that I could not truly understand what these women felt until I 'got it.') My getting it came through my care and concern for them as individuals.... That moment, which I spoke on in class as it was happening, allowed me to openly admit my deficiency in that area. It gave me a new charge in my life ... one that I am still coming to grips with and constantly working on. It is my duty to be protector and provider.

Speaking to the use of the genogram the following comments were expressed:

"My family was not close to my mother's side of the family, but as I did the genogram I had a desire to know my grandmother

CONCLUSION

and my aunts. I want to know their story because it's a part of my own story. So this past Christmas at my brother's wedding I began those relationships. It's only the beginning, but I am excited at the possibility."

"Participation in the class kind of confirmed what I already knew about my family. However, seeing it in a visual (genogram) was striking. At one point, I couldn't figure out how to map the various relationships. They were simply too many but all have had an impact on me individually and the family as a whole."

Recognizing and understanding generational trauma were described in the following statements.

"I am a social worker with a background in post-traumatic stress disorder. As such, I am able to fairly easily connect traumatic experiences to behavior and family patterns. What was an eye opener for me is the ancestral trauma that many of us are still carrying around based, not on stories about slavery, but due to the actual experiences that our ancestors had. In other words, I unknowingly carry around the trauma experienced by my grandmother that she never even talked about."

"My relationship and discussions with my son have shifted. He and many of his friends have grown up without the presence of their father and information from this class helps me to explain possible generational trauma which could have contributed to their scarred behaviors."

The use of the genogram and how it informs prayers were expressed in the following descriptions:

"My prayers are now more clearly directed for my family now. When I see the pattern being manifested, I pray for the breaking of the bond/pattern and for healing the woundedness."

"I experienced the realization that issues and traumatic experiences can manifest in a spiritual entity that can be acknowledged, addressed, and prayed for, not only praying for myself but for the issue. . . . Now prayer for the issue is detached from a specific person."

"In talking with my father, in particular, I've been more aware of how I should intercede on his behalf. Our conversations have

Part I

revealed the need for him to forgive and let some things go. I can see more clearly places of being 'stuck.' If anything, knowing specifically how to pray for myself as well as my extended family is now a focus. I feel as though I am engaged in spiritually tearing down strongholds. I wish others in the family would join me, but I suppose that will come."

Responses to the healing service:

"I thoroughly enjoyed the healing service. It was both raw and honest. Things that were on our minds that would never be said in traditional "Christian" settings were shared. God already knew so it was no revelation for God, but an opportunity for us to both lament and celebrate. I didn't read my lament during the service, but certainly did write one and enjoyed the service."

"The healing service was a very personal and reflective event for me.... You seldom get a chance to use a stretch of time to ponder, to reflect and to experience transformation in your everyday life. I felt that the service was very much a process of closure and an opening of the spirit to embrace a new beginning of life experiences. I find myself very emotional and compassionate to concerns that surround me after class."

Descriptions of the overall experience were described as images by two of the participants:

"A treasure chest. It's been more than a light bulb experience but more like opening a treasure chest."

"I envision the statue of Booker T Washington where he uncovers/enlightens a kneeling Black individual, that represents the spirit of Black people (I've also heard that some people interpreted him as covering up blacks). I feel that our class has for me uncovered/enlightened me to the view of the history of my family tree in a very uplifting and positive way."

One of the most profound statements made in the class in response to the question "What was your experience of the healing service?"

"I am the hope and dream of a slave."

Also expressed in the conversation in class was the increased interest in history. Not only African American history, but history in general; and listening with curiosity as to where African American history connects.

CONCLUSION

For example, one person listening to a lecture about the history of Jewish immigration to New York between 1840 and 1920, made the connection of the Jewish garment industry clothing slaves for sale during the domestic slave trade. Another person realized watching the *Slavery by Another Name* documentary that his family had moved from Alabama to West Virginia and were part of the industrial slavery system in the coal mines.

The oldest member of the class expressed gratitude in being included even though it was evident that she was grieving the loss of untold stories in her family because there were so few family members left to tell it and she, at eighty, was one of them and knew so little. Another member of the class identified generational trauma in her pastor's family and recognized how it was being passed down in the church. She chose to move to another church that provided opportunities for the growth of all church members.

Healing happens in many ways. There can be profound and transformational healing through reading, sharing, and conversation. This class was a "head and heart" class. It was so successful because it was a homogenous group in the most important ways. They were African American Christians with compatible organic and academic intelligence who respected each other, and no one was a complete stranger. One of the participants commented on how wonderful it was to have such intense and deep discussion with such a compatible yet diverse group.

SELF-DISCOVERY

It was advised to freewrite as soon as possible after each class. The classes were physically and emotionally exhausting, therefore writing was only the required fifteen minutes on the night of the class and then augmented the notes the following morning. These notes were very helpful in capturing the mood of the class.

There were three new discoveries working with this subject matter. First was the size and economic power of the domestic slave trade. The total dollar value of enslaved African Americans in the South, expressed in historical dollars and controlled for inflation, generally represented a full one-third or more of all the liquid capital in the entire South. Slaves were the single largest financial asset in the United States—worth over $3.5 billion in 1860 dollars ($97.65 billion in today's dollars)—more than the values of the railroads, banks, factories, and ships combined. The realization

PART I

of those facts made war inevitable. Only something as destructive as war could break the stronghold of economic greed and power.

Second was the importance of communal mourning. The Jewish, Armenian, and Native American cultures have rituals of mourning imbedded in their cultural history. Jews commemorate the victims of the Holocaust on Yom Hashoah, the 27th day of Nissan in the Jewish calendar, held this year on April 15th (2015). Armenians set aside an annual "Day of Mourning and Commemoration" for the victims of the genocide on April 24th. Native Americans' Day of Mourning is the same as the American celebration of Thanksgiving. Native Americans mourn those who have suffered the theft of their lands and the destruction of their traditional way of life at the hands of the American nation.

The International Day of Remembrance of the Victims of Slavery and the Transatlantic Slave Trade was initiated by the United Nations in 1997. The date selected was March 25, the date the transatlantic slave trade ended in Britain. "The Ark of Return" memorial was dedicated on the grounds of the United Nations March 25, 2015. However, this day of remembrance is practically unknown in the African American community.[1] Mourning was, and still is, expressed in the music. It began with the sorrow and work songs of the enslaved. The songs were passed down from generation to generation to enable the expression of the pain and sorrow to be continual, spontaneous and impromptu because of the conditions of chronic condemnation and persistent peril in which the African Americans lived. Since emancipation, this form of mourning has continued and evolved over time. Mourning songs are found in the rap music of today, and these songs join those other songs in the blues, freedom songs, rhythm and blues, jazz, gospel genre. Through their faith and their music, African Americans have grappled constructively with transgenerational trauma. More intentional healing rituals like communal mourning and laments will enhance their resilience and wellness.

Third, besides seeking freedom, seeking family was of equal motivation for runaways. The likelihood of finding their family members was slim. There must have been an elaborate communication network, coupled with an inordinate hope that motivated them to seek their family members.

---

1. United Nations, "Permanent Memorial to Honour the Victims of Slavery and the Transatlantic Slave Trade at the United Nations," http://www.un.org/en/events/slavery-remembranceday/memorial.shtml.

CONCLUSION
FUTURE CONSIDERATION

The knowledge gained from teaching the class allowed a portion of history's invisible text to become visible. Racism and its economic relationship are deeply embedded in the American national psyche. Understanding the sources and seminal events that produced patterns of relationships, behavior, and attitudes that are observed today reduces stress with the realization that this drama will continue to play itself out with new variations until the cycle is broken. The Sankofa bird, whose body is heading in one direction and whose head is turned in the opposite direction, means "we cannot go forward without first looking back to our past to understand how we have gotten to where we are." This class is the beginning of a new work that will contribute to the healing of past, current and future generations.

PART II

Roots Matter: Healing History, Honoring Heritage, Renewing Hope

LEADER'S GUIDE

Introduction

PRELIMINARY PREPARATIONS

This manual is designed to be a guide for leading the program, "Roots Matter." This course will teach the impact of transgenerational trauma on families and identify ways to foster healing for the present and future generations.

The course objectives are for the participants to: a) understand the lasting effects of trauma; b) recognize the importance of family history and how it influences the present; c) appreciate the resiliency of the human spirit and the healing power of faith and prayer; d) design a spiritual discipline to facilitate healing of transgenerational trauma in the African American church community.

There are several ways to schedule this course. Frequency can be monthly or weekly, and the format can be retreat only, retreat/class combination or class only. This course assumes that the members are mostly self-directed adults. However, it can be offered as an intergenerational project. Because of the sensitive and emotional nature of the subject material, consideration should be given to the appropriateness of the material based on age and emotional maturity.

Inviting participants

You may be leading a course that has been publicized and has been filled through a registration process.

Part II: Leader's Guide

If you want to choose the participants for the program, see the sample letter of invitation for ideas on how to approach members of the community.

Suggestions for preparing for the course

Classroom or teaching space size should be accessible (on the first floor or near an elevator) and near bathrooms. The classroom should facilitate intimacy but not seem overcrowded. It should be well lit and ventilated. If using A/V equipment, make sure it is available and working.

Parking should be convenient and well lit. Providing escorts for the participants to their cars is an alternative.

Providing food and supervised childcare reduce barriers for participation in the course, especially if the course is offered in the evenings. Both should be in convenient proximity to the classroom.

If food is provided, consider assistance in purchase, storage, prep space and set-up. Also consider access to the kitchen/prep space/classroom before and after class for setup and cleanup.

If you have a large number of participants, form discussion groups of no less than three persons, but no more than five persons. The ideal group size for discussion is four or five individuals.

Because the topics of discussion can be personal and sensitive, consider beginning the learning experience with a class covenant or consent form. (See samples.) This practice can help establish trust and set ground rules for confidentiality. Review the course syllabus in the first session to explain and clarify requirements and expectations.

To bring closure to the course, allow time for members to complete and discuss the evaluation of the course. (See Appendix D.) Plan for decorations and special materials for the healing service. Consider a token gift or certificate.

Determine how the financial expenses will be covered for the notebooks, CDs, DVDs, books, copying, meeting space, refreshments, and childcare. (See Table 1.)

Assignment prior to the first session

In order to set the tone and focus of the course, it is both time and cost efficient to assign a class related activity to be completed before the participants come to the first session. A week after the close of registration, send a confirmation correspondence to the registrants. (See the sample confirmation email.) If the start date is more than two weeks out, send a separate email two weeks before the start date with the following instructions. If the start date of the course is two weeks or less, include the instructions in the confirmation correspondence.

Instructions:

Request that they find a prayer partner, or someone they can trust with their own personal and confidential material for processing.

Request that they gather family stories and give the website link to assist them in ways to ask questions. (See the first session assignment in the sample email text.)

Part II: Leader's Guide

SAMPLE INVITATION LETTER

This letter is an invitation to participate in the Roots Matter program.

There will be six weekly two hour sessions. All will be held on (day) ___ from (time) ___ to (time) ___. The dates are ___ to ___. The sessions will be held at (location) _____

Participants in the program will 1) become knowledgeable of trauma and transgenerational trauma literature; 2) identify biblical themes and theological concepts of trauma, suffering, forgiveness, and healing; 3) investigate the role of intercessory prayer in the generational healing process; 4) create a genogram using either a stencil template or genogram software of at least three generations of family members; 5) design individually and collectively healing rituals and prayers; 6) participate in a closing generational healing service.

Because of the emotional nature of the material and for the well-being of the participants, attendance at all sessions is seriously and earnestly recommended. *If you are interested and have the time to participate, please respond to this email or call me at _____ by _____.*

I am excited about this program, and I look forward to learning with you.

'till earth and heaven ring!

SAMPLE CONFIRMATION EMAIL

Hello everyone,

There are sixteen of you who have agreed to participate in this project. Thank you! There is one participant who does not use email, but the rest of you can see who your colleagues will be from the distribution list. I know it will be a positive learning and healing experience for me, and I hope it will be for you as well.

I have ordered some materials and will be preparing more as we get closer to our start date. Please let me know if your plans change and you cannot participate.

All sessions will be held on (day) ___ from (time) ___ to (time) ___. The dates are ____ to ____. The sessions will be held at (location) _____.

Look for another email from me in late ____ or early _____.

I pray your summer is all you expect.

'till earth and heaven ring!

Part II: Leader's Guide

SAMPLE EMAIL TEXT

To be sent two weeks prior to the start of the course

Hello everyone,

I hope you had a good summer. I have been preparing for our co-learning experience and look forward to seeing you in _____. To prepare for our time together, I am asking you to do a few things.

First, I ask that you find someone to pray with and for you and your family. One of the things I have become acutely aware of is how important family and freedom were to our ancestors. At least one third of the runaways were trying to visit family. Many of those who escaped would risk going back to get family members. Those who bought their freedom usually stayed close by in order to buy their family members. That is what happened in my family. In some ways we are taking on the role of freeing our families as we intercede for them.

Second, I ask that you begin to gather your family stories. They will help you begin identifying the transgenerational trauma that needs healing and the triumphs that need celebrating. I am including this link to the StoryCorps website: http://storycorps.org/great-questions/. Pick any five (5) that appeal to you. Write your answers and the reasons why you chose the five you selected. I will ask you to share one from your list before the end of our first session. Make two (2) copies, one to turn in to me, and one to keep.

Finally, I am organizing materials and planning light refreshments for the program. Please let me know by _____ if your circumstances have changed, and if you will not be able to participate. The latest count is fifteen. As a reminder:

Dates:
Time:
Location:

See you in two weeks.

'till earth and heaven ring!

ROOTS MATTER: HEALING HISTORY,
HONORING HERITAGE, RENEWING HOPE

Session One

Family Systems and the Genogram

Part II: leader's guide

SESSION ONE

Introduction

The insights, memories, emotions, and experiences that this course will yield can be life-changing. Therefore, it is important to set the tone of your time together. Take the time to allow members to introduce themselves during this first formal study session. Use the icebreaker activity as a way to help members relax, open up, and begin sharing personal information in a non-threatening way.

Objectives

The three objectives for this session are:

- members will be welcomed and introduced with name stories
- members will be presented with the course structure
- members will clarify expectations and responsibilities

Preparation

- Read and complete the activities in *A Family Genogram Workbook* before leading this session. This will familiarize you with the content and enable you to answer questions raised by the participants throughout the session.
- Purchase a copy of the book and a template for each participant. (optional)
- Update the consent form. (See Appendix A.)
- Update the syllabus with the session dates. (See Appendix B.)
- Provide each participant with a notebook with copies of the consent form/covenant and syllabus.
- Gather tent cards and markers.
- Bring a copy of *Prayers for Dark People* by W. E. B. Dubois or other devotional material for the opening prayer.
- Bring freewrite questions for in-class activity.

Family Systems and the Genogram

Session Outline

1. Welcome participants as they come in and direct them to the classroom, the food, if provided, childcare and locations of the bathrooms. If the members of the group are new to each other, or if there are visitors to a session, distribute name tags to help the members get to know each other easier.

2. As part of their introductions, ask them to tell the story about their name. Were they named after someone? Who named them? Does their name have a meaning? Does their name have a story?

3. Open the session with prayer. Give a brief welcome and purpose of the program and a brief outline of the session. Begin the introductions exercise. Start with yourself to model what is expected. Sign your name on the tent card with the marker, and pass the tent cards and marker to the next person.

4. Distribute the notebooks. Review the consent form or covenant. There should be two copies, one to turn in and one to keep. Have the participants read it out loud and ask questions. Ask each member to sign and turn in the consent form.

5. Review the syllabus that includes a general class outline, a definition of cinquain and freewrite exercises, and weekly offerings. Bring an offering to share with them and explain why it is important to you. Be sure to ask if there are questions as you move through the material.

6. After the ten minute break, begin with the homework of sharing family stories. Then distribute copies of A Family Genogram Workbook and template to each participant. These will be their personal copies. Direct the participants to begin working on their own genogram at home and continue to work on it throughout the duration of the course.

7. Introduce the topic "The Genogram and Family Systems." Distribute the topic handout.

8. Direct the participants to write a freewrite about what has happened in class so far. Have volunteers read what they have written.

9. Give the assignment before dismissing. Distribute the freewrite questions. Tell the participants that the following article is recommended additional reading: "Genogram and African American Families:

PART II: LEADER'S GUIDE

Employing Strengths of Spirituality, Religion, and Extended Family Network" by Annie McCullough Chavis. Remind them to start working on their genogram.

10. Close with prayer.

FAMILY SYSTEMS AND THE GENOGRAM

LESSON PLAN: SESSION ONE

Orientation

Family Systems and the Genogram

Objectives

- To understand how the session is structured
- To identify participant expectations
- To explain participant responsibilities

Note: This schedule assumes a session is from 6:30—8:30 p.m.

Time	Activity	Leader Resources	References or Handouts for participants
6:30 (5 min.)	Welcome Opening prayer Bathrooms, start/stop, notes, birthdays	*Prayers for Dark People*—WEB Dubois	
6:35 (5 min.)	Purpose Session outline What/How/Why	Session outline & notes	
6:40 (15 min.)	Introductions—What is your name? Who named you? Why? What does your name mean? Is it a family name? How do you feel about your name? What do you want to be called?	Tent cards and markers	

Part II: Leader's Guide

Time	Activity	Leader Resources	References or Handouts for participants
6:55 (20 min.)	Distribute notebooks and review: Consent form Syllabus Cinquain Freewrite Freewrite exercise Offerings for the Healing Service	Freewrite exercise question: What impression or feelings do you have about what has happened so far in this session? 2 min. 2–3 volunteers to share	Notebooks contain: Consent form Syllabus Freewrite instructions Cinquain instructions Offering explanation
7:15 (10 min.)	Break		
7:25 (20 min.)	StoryCorps activity	Share 1 of 5 selected questions	Have members share 1 of 5 questions; turn in all 5
7:45 (20 min.)	Family Systems & Genogram Workbook		Genogram workbook & template Topic handout
8:05 (15 min.)	Freewrite Question 1		
8:20	Assignments: Begin work on genogram Freewrite questions Offering		Freewrite questions
	Closing Prayer		

FAMILY SYSTEMS AND THE GENOGRAM

Murray Bowen, M.D., 1913–1990 was a pioneer in family therapy and a developer of a systems theory of the family. Bowen perceived families as systems of interconnected and interdependent individuals, none of whom could be understood in isolation from one another, but rather as a part of a larger group emotional unit.

A family system is the manner in which a group of people, related by blood, marriage or fictive kinship, function in relationship to each other wherein they develop patterns of behavior that are caused by or causes other family members to act in predictable ways. Maintaining the same pattern of relationships can lead to both healthy and unhealthy behavior. Fictive kinship is a term used to describe the kinds of social ties and relationships that are very often not necessarily based on blood ties or marriage ties, but may rather be based on shared residence, shared economic ties, or familiarity via other forms of interaction.

There are eight interlocking concepts in Bowen's theory: triangles, nuclear family emotional system, family projection process, societal emotional process, emotional cutoff, sibling position, differentiation of self, and multigenerational transmission process. The scope of this program will focus on two of Bowen's concepts: differentiation of self and multigenerational transmission process. For further reading, see www.thebowencenter.org.

Differentiation of self is the ability to single out one's personhood from the group by drawing distinctions between self and others because there is an innate desire to become authentic individuals. The basic building blocks of a "self" are inborn, but an individual's family relationships during childhood and adolescence primarily determine how much "self" he or she develops. Once established, the level of "self" rarely changes unless a person makes a structured and long-term effort to change it. Bowen identifies four main types of differentiation: 1) low—People of low differentiation have very little sense of self outside the relationship system. They are people pleasers who spend all their energy seeking approval and acceptance. 2) moderate—People who are guided by accepted tradition and law. Lacking a solid "self" conviction about the world, they will often quote "rules" and "scientific fact" to make their point. 3) good—Those who can hold their own under "peer" pressure, who can participate in emotional relationships with confidence and have the ability to remove themselves if the need arises. 4) high—Bowen considers people with high differentiation as more hypothetical than real. It is more what he or she is not. They are not the "rugged individualist" which he describes as a "pretend" posture of those who are fighting against the "system." These persons are always aware of others and the relationships around them. However, they recognize their dependence on others. Confident in their thinking, they can either support another's view without being a disciple or reject another's view without polarizing the differences.

The *multigenerational transmission process* describes how small differences in the levels of differentiation between parents and their offspring lead to marked differences over many generations among the members of a multigenerational family. Relationally and genetically transmitted information interacts to shape an individual's "self." The combination of parents actively shaping the development of their offspring, offspring innately responding to their parents' moods, attitudes, and actions, and the long dependency period of human offspring results in people developing levels of differentiation of self, similar to their parents' levels. However, the relationship patterns of nuclear family emotional systems often result in at least one member of a sibling group developing a little more "self" and another member developing a little less "self" than the parents.

Genograms were first developed by Murray Bowen in the 1970's and popularized in clinical settings by Monica McGoldrick and Randy Gerson through the publication of *Genograms: Assessment and Intervention* in 1985. The book was updated in 1999 and 2008 to define new family relationships such as blended families, extended families to include pets, caregivers, fictive kinship, and relationships in the LGBT community. The Genogram is a pictorial display in which physical, psychological, spiritual, behavioral hereditary patterns are visualized and identified because of a systematic method of recording family history and relationships. The genogram maps out relationships and traits that may otherwise be missed on a family tree.

Genogram Clues

Dates—provide information that helps put events in perspective. They indicate what else might have been going on simultaneously or what a certain sequence of experiences might have been, e.g., a family has three significant losses within a year.

Gender—Beliefs and values may thread through families in powerful and subtle ways, creating difficulties when a member marries someone with different gender beliefs, e.g., men are involved in sports and women should support them.

Secrets—unrevealed or unknown to some, secrets provide information about the boundaries and communication patterns in certain families. Secrets can have positive and negative effects.

Losses—critical illness, death, disabilities, economic reversals, job losses, miscarriages, divorces. The question to ask is to what extent was this event perceived as a loss.

Themes—speak to the questions "Who are we"? "How do we behave"? They make evident the families belief structure and guide the family in future behavior, e.g., an engaged couple has conflict over expectations around home and career. He comes from a home where all the male members are the major breadwinner and the wives stay at home. She comes from a home in which she was encouraged to be independent and self-sufficient or vice versa.

Positive Patterns and Traits: Special Gifts, Talents, Blessings

Identify by name, if possible, the people in your family who have or had:

- musical talent for singing, playing an instrument, dancing
- artistic talent, e.g., painting, sculpture
- writing talent
- cooking talent
- fashion design talent

Part II: Leader's Guide

- craft making talent
- technical skills
- an interest in recording family history
- an interest in volunteering and community service
- the gift of hospitality
- an exceptional gift of faith
- the gift of intercessory prayer
- the gift of stewardship
- entrepreneurial skills

Identify by name, if possible, people in your family who valued:

- family
- education
- technology
- environment
- life-long learning

Identify by name, if possible, people in your family who were:

- faithful in their relationships
- stable providers
- compassionate listeners
- deeply spiritual
- loved children
- liked and respected by family and community

Suggestions for drawing your genogram

If you are not familiar with the genogram, read the introduction and chapter 1 in *A Family Genogram Workbook* before starting.

Give yourself time to work on it. You may have to stop and google or call somebody to get an answer to a question that surfaces. You may be surprised how much you know, thought you knew or don't know.

Use removable scotch tape to add or adjust paper as your genogram expands (and it will) or a large roll of paper.

Redraw with the template or software after you feel it is pretty stable.

There may be resistance and/or distractions from yourself as well as family members. Pray for revelation of what the cause may be.

There are suggestions on how to ask questions in the workbook and on the StoryCorps website.
Keep in mind the generational patterns; the goal is not to blame but to explain.

This is an ongoing project that will be filled in over time.

Part II: Leader's Guide

FREEWRITE HOMEWORK QUESTIONS

Session One: Family History and the Genogram

Session Questions

The first question was the question you started in class. You can complete it or choose another question. You can answer all three if you choose. Make two copies of your freewriting, one to turn in and one to contribute to the class discussion.

1) Think about a family gathering when stories were shared about the lives of family members. What was it about the telling of the family stories that you found interesting?

2) How might you create an environment that helps young and old alike to feel comfortable talking about gifts, graces, talents, and resiliency of parents, grandparents, and great-grandparents? What might you pay more attention to if you plan story-sharing at the next family gathering?

3) What can you do to make the space comfortable, inviting and more hospitable when it comes to using the genogram to identify family patterns of negative characteristics, bad behaviors, and patterns of illness in the family? How would you invite the sharing of memories from a diversity of perspectives and/or mixture of voices from the youngest to the oldest?

Additional Reading: Annie McCullough Chavis, "Genograms and African American Families: Employing Family Strengths, Religion, and Extended Family Networks," *Michigan Family Review* 9, no. 1 (2004): 30–36.

Please pick and elaborate on at least one of the three article related statements. You can respond to all three if you choose. Make two copies of the freewrite — one to turn in and one to contribute to the class discussion.

1) My thoughts after reading this article are . . .

2) Having read this article, I would like to know more about . . .

3) Questions that came to mind as I read this article were . . .

Don't forget to bring your weekly offering!!!!

ROOTS MATTER: HEALING HISTORY,
HONORING HERITAGE, RENEWING HOPE

Session Two

Old Testament and Family Stories

Part II: leader's guide

SESSION TWO

Introduction

The second session will focus on the biblical story of Patriarchs Abraham, Isaac and Jacob, looking at them from a family systems perspective. There will also be a study of the references to generational blessings and curses in scripture.

Objectives

The two objectives for this session are:

- To identify scripture references to generational blessings and curses
- To illustrate positive and negative traits of Abraham's family

Preparation

- A copy of *Prayers for Dark People* by W. E. B. Dubois or other devotional material for the opening prayer
- *Africans in America* DVD
- A/V equipment in working order
- Offering
- Abraham family genogram
- Session topic handout
- Homework freewrite questions

Session Outline

1. As part of the devotional exercise and after the opening prayer, have the participants watch chapters 2 and 3 of *Africans in America*. Direct the participants to write a cinquain on what they watched. Close the devotional exercise by having the participants read their cinquains. End each reading with the phrase "ashe (ah-shay)—let it be so."

Old Testament and Family Stories

2. Have participants report about progress with their genogram—questions, insights, experiences, obstacles.

3. Open the discussion about last week's topic or questions.

4. After the break, have the participants share their offerings for the week. Ask them to pass around their offerings after sharing their story.

5. Display the Abraham family genogram and explain the relationships and patterns from generation to generation. Distribute handout of weekly topic.

6. Assignment: before dismissing, distribute the freewrite questions. Collect the homework freewrites.

7. Close with prayer.

Part II: leader's guide

LESSON PLAN: SESSION TWO

Old Testament Family Stories

Objectives

- To identify Scripture that references generational blessings and curses
- To illustrate positive and negative traits of Abraham's family

Note: This schedule assumes a session is from 6:30—8:30 p.m.

Time	Activity	Leader Resources	References and Handouts for Participants
	Turn in freewrite and cinquain		
6:30 (10 min.)	Opening prayer Video clip	*Prayers for Dark People*—W. E. B. Dubois DVD: *Africans in America*, chapters 2 & 3	
6:40 (10 min.)	Cinquain devotional		
6:50 (10 min.)	Genogram check-in Experiences, insights, obstacles, etc.		
7:00 (30 min.)	Freewrite on session		
7:30 (10 min.)	Break		
7:40 (20 min.)	Offerings		
8:00 (25 min.)	OT Family Stories Genogram		Topic handout

Old Testament and Family Stories

Time	Activity	Leader Resources	References and Handouts for Participants
8:25	Assignments: Freewrite questions		Freewrite questions
	Closing Prayer		

Part II: leader's guide

OLD TESTAMENT AND NEW TESTAMENT

Family Relationships

Dr. Robert Sears SJ studied theology and psychotherapy at Fordham University and received his doctorate in 1974. He is an adjunct professor at Loyola University's Institute of Pastoral Studies and Superior of its Gonzaga Jesuit Community. Since 1981, Sears has been a member of the Association of Christian Therapists (ACT) where he currently serves as board chaplain. Sears raises and answers this question in his article "Healing and Family Spiritual/Emotional Systems." What is the interdependence between generations and how are we freed from the negative patterns for new life in Christ?

Old Testament

Sears identifies three key attributes in the family relationships of the Israelites. As African Americans we have the same three attributes in our family relationships: 1) corporate personality, 2) the Old Testament formula: "Unto the fourth generation," and 3) the recognition of individual responsibility.

Corporate personality extends beyond the present to the past and future. Ancestors and contemporaries are seen as one family. The Patriarchs Abraham, Isaac and Jacob are unifying presences in the nation that carries their name, honor, and life. As Jacob ages he says "I am to be gathered unto my kindred" Gn 4:21; Amos speaks of his contemporaries as "the whole family which I brought up out of the land of Egypt" (Am 3:1). In the African American community the unifying presence would be that of Nat Turner, Harriet Tubman, Sojurnerer Truth, and Frederick Douglass.

The unity of individual and community can be concentrated in a single representative. It is more than a moral bond; it is real as blood ties, unconscious instinctive bonding, e.g., David and Goliath are Israel and the Philistines; Joe Louis and Max Schmeling; Obama and Romney, a fluid passing from individual to collective and vice versa as though each was seen in the other. The "suffering servant" of second Isaiah is both singular and plural. The situation in which you represent yourself and your "race" such as being the only one in the class, board meeting, PTA meeting, etc.

The leader is a representative of the group as intercessor as well as an individual, e.g., Moses and the prophets, Malcolm X and Martin Luther King Jr., Barack and Michelle Obama.

Unto the fourth generation referred to in the scripture: "I the LORD your God am a jealous God visiting the iniquity of the fathers upon the children to the third and fourth generation but showing steadfast love to thousands of those who love me and keep my commandments" (Ex: 20:5–6; 34:6–8; Numbers 14:18; Dt. 5:1–10) This notion is especially important for understanding the transference of generational patterns. In the pre-exilic texts the family head was seen in his offspring, not only for blessing as with Abraham and his offspring (Gn. 12:1–3; 22:15- 18), but also for punishment as when David took a census of the people and all Israel was punished (2 Sam. 24:15–17).

Individual responsibility: The exile released for Israel a new sense of individual responsibility. Ezekiel has Yahweh repeal the saying about the fathers eating sour grapes and setting the children's teeth on edge (Ez. 18).

Each is rewarded or punished according to his or her own choices. What is affirmed is the freedom to repent. Only the one who sins will be punished. . . . It was not to be understood as only one choice, the father's, but the sons and offspring also have sinned by following his example. Paul later shows the same understanding regarding the sin of Adam. "Sin came into the world through one man and death through sin . . . and so death spread to all men because all men sinned." (Rom. 5:12). Children are conditioned by their parents' choices but they also choose consciously or unconsciously, and so on down the generations. Example: husband/wife relationships of Abraham and Isaac are similar; Jacob learned trickery from his mother. God's response to this network of sin was to affirm the possibility of individual repentance. To enable that He promises to take over himself (see Ez. 34), to put his Spirit in their hearts and make them keep his commands (Ez. 36:24–28; Jer. 31:31–34). Individual freedom is grounded in a personal relationship with God.

Part II: leader's guide

New Testament

Jesus breaks tradition and teaches disciples to leave family for the sake of the tradition (Mk 10:28–30). Jesus separates himself from his family and tells his followers they will have to do the same because it is about being differentiated from his family and centering exclusively on God . . . the ultimate in relationships. Both Matthew and Luke portray Jesus' virginal conception as a "new beginning" through the creative power of the Spirit, and Jesus' differentiated relationship to the Father ultimately leads to his separation from even close ties of relationships when he is abandoned on the cross. He is called to a total centering on God.

Jesus is linked to the history of the people, not the immediate family. Matthew takes him back to Abraham; Luke takes him back to Adam. The temptations in the wilderness are tests to differentiate from human relationships. Matthew sees Jesus as Moses, Priest and King and the temptations are to feed people (Moses), do miracles (Priest), rule (King). Luke sees him as Messiah. Jesus bears the weight of his tradition but responds in a new way in total fidelity to his Father.

Jesus is head of a new people. Jesus heads the community of the people of the spirit. Jesus frees us from familial and national bonds to create a new people. The connection is not the law but something greater, the Holy Spirit. Connection by the Holy Spirit supersedes the power of the law but in following the Holy Spirit the law is automatically fulfilled. For Paul, Jesus is the new Adam (1 Cor. 15:45). For Luke, Jesus is the Messiah (Acts 2:32–36). For John, Jesus is the Word who was with the Father in the beginning, and to all who believe in him he gave power to become "children of God" (the new community) (John 1:12). Jesus' (and our) freeing from familial relationships is not to lead to isolation but to creativity in bringing about a new community in the Spirit. As we differentiate from our families through prayer for the ancestors we influence the families to become part of a healed and renewed community. . . . The pattern is separation from natural ties, new centering in Jesus' Spirit, and renewal of spiritual community.

OLD TESTAMENT FAMILY STORIES

Scripture identifies and supports the transmission of positive traits (blessings) and negative traits (curses) through the generations. Curses are those negative traits and circumstances that occur because of poor choices and disobedience. Blessings are those positive traits and circumstances that occur because of good choices, inherited skills, gifts, talents and grace.

Examples of the belief in the transmission of blessing and curses are found in 1) Exodus 20: 5-6—You shall not bow down to them (idols) or worship them; for I the LORD your God am a jealous God, punishing children for the iniquity of parents, to the third and the fourth generation of those who reject me, but showing love to a thousand generations of those who love me and keep my commandments. And, 2) Psalm 103:17-18—But from everlasting to everlasting the LORD's love is with those who fear him, and his righteousness with their children's children with those who keep his covenant and remember to obey his precepts.

Examples of generational blessings can be found in Genesis 48:15-16 when Israel (Jacob) blesses Joseph's sons, Ephraim and Manasseh. "He blessed Joseph, and said, The God before whom my ancestors Abraham and Isaac walked, the God who has been my shepherd all my life to this day, the angel who has redeemed me from all harm, bless the boys; and in them let my name be perpetuated, and the name of my ancestors Abraham and Isaac; and let them grow into a multitude on the earth."

Isaiah prophesies to the exiles a blessing in Isaiah 44:1-5 "But now hear, O Jacob my servant, Israel whom I have chosen! Thus says the LORD who made you, who formed you in the womb and will help you: Do not fear, O Jacob my servant, Israel whom I have chosen. For I will pour water on the thirsty land, and streams on the dry ground; I will pour my spirit upon your descendants, and my blessing on your offspring. They shall spring up like a green tamarisk, like willows by flowing streams. This one will say, 'I am the LORD's,' another will be called by the name of Jacob, yet another will write on the hand, 'The LORD's,' and adopt the name of Israel."

In 2 Timothy 1:3-5 Paul recognized Timothy's gift of faith passed on from grandmother to mother to son. "I am grateful to God—whom I worship with a clear conscience, as my ancestors did—when I remember you constantly in my prayers night and day. Recalling your tears, I long to see you so that I may be filled with joy. I am reminded of your sincere faith, a faith that lived first in your grandmother, Lois, and your mother, Eunice, and now, I am sure, lives in you."

Examples of the transmission of generational patterns can be identified in the family and descendants of Abraham and Sarah. However, one must keep in mind that we are reading into this story our twenty-first-century interpretation of what transpired. Timeframe and culture greatly influenced their behavior and influence ours, but there are some basic family relationships that are common, if not universal and timeless.

The First Generation—Abram and Sarai—Genesis 16:1–16; 17:15–22; 21:1–21

In this family narrative, Sarai, Abram's wife, cannot conceive and takes matters in her own hands and has Abraham sleep with Hagar, her maidservant. Sarai and Hagar have a hostile relationship after Ishmael is born and Hagar runs away. God sends her back with a promise of Ishmael becoming the father of many descendants. Sarai favors Isaac because he is her biological child. Abram wanted Ishmael to be an equal part of the family, but Sarai would not allow it. Isaac's birth was celebrated but not Ishmael's. There is favoritism of the younger child, and the favoritism triggers sibling rivalry. Sarai, believing that Isaac's blessing and inheritance are threatened, forces Hagar and Ishmael out of the family home. Abram, a father who did not stand by Ishmael in times of dispute, diminishes Ishmael's sense of self-worth and poisons his future relationships with his father and Isaac.

The Second Generation—Isaac and Rebekah—Genesis 24; 25:19–34; 27:41–45; 33:1, 12–20

Rebekah, Isaac's wife, has difficulty conceiving but eventually gives birth to twin boys. Isaac favors Esau, the older twin and Rebekah favors Jacob, the younger twin. Sibling rivalry surfaces again between Jacob and Esau, and they become pawns in the parental struggle over the inheritance—the same struggle as between Ishmael and Isaac in the previous generation. At his mother's prompting, Jacob tricks Esau and his father into receiving the blessing of the first born son. Isaac's history is repeated in Jacob, the mother's favorite wins. Jacob, the younger child, is forced to leave home. The reason is different; Jacob stole Esau's inheritance rather than being denied an inheritance like Ishmael, but the struggle was again over the inheritance.

The Third Generation—Jacob and Rachel—Genesis 29:16–28; 29:31–30:25; 35:16–20; 37:17b-28

In the third generation trickery is repeated. Jacob tricks Laban into an agreement that results in his getting the better flocks of sheep and goats. Jacob is tricked by his father-in-law, Laban, into marrying Leah, his older daughter, and into working seven more years in order to marry Rachel, the younger daughter whom Jacob really loved. There is tension between Rachel and Leah, like Sarah and Hagar, in the competition of childbirth which included the maidservants. Jacob favors Rachel and her children, Joseph and Benjamin. Sibling rivalry occurs among the other brothers. Joseph, the oldest son of Rachel, is sold into slavery, and once again a child is forced to leave home.

In light of Bowen's family systems theory, what do these family group stories say about relationships between husband and wife, father and son, mother and son, siblings relationships and marriage?

PART II: LEADER'S GUIDE

FREEWRITE HOMEWORK QUESTIONS

Session Two: Old Testament Stories

Session Questions

The first question was the question you started in class. You can complete it or choose another question. You can answer all three if you choose. Make two copies of your freewrite, one to turn in and one to contribute to the class discussion.

1) What biblical stories about generational blessings and curses have been a help to you?
2) What scripture lessons have you heard about but not studied, that if you did study, might make your family situation better?
3) What are some of your favorite hymns, spirituals, and gospel music that you turn to when healing is needed?

Pick and elaborate on at least one statement. You can respond to all three if you choose. Make two copies of your freewrite, one to turn in and one to contribute to the class discussion.

1) My thoughts after reading this article are . . .
2) Having read this article, I would like to know more about . . .
3) Questions that came to mind as I read this article were . . .

Don't forget to bring your weekly offering!!!!!

ROOTS MATTER: HEALING HISTORY,
HONORING HERITAGE, RENEWING HOPE

Session Three

Generational Trauma in Jewish, Armenian, and Native American History

Part II: leader's guide

SESSION THREE

Introduction

During this session the participants will hear personal stories from two speakers who have worked on their genograms and participated in a healing service for their families. The participants will also be introduced to research on generational trauma in other cultures.

If no speakers are available, you can share your own personal experience or those of others who have given you permission to share, or follow the outline of Session Two for the first hour. Be sure to select a video clip to use in the devotional.

Objectives

The two objectives for this session are:

- To introduce speakers to tell of their experiences and insights working on their family genogram
- To introduce current research studies on trauma and generational trauma in the Jewish, Armenian, and Native American history

Preparation

- A copy of *Prayers for Dark People* by W. E. B. Dubois or other devotional material for the opening prayer
- Offering
- Topic handout
- Homework freewrite questions

Session Outline

1. Begin the session with prayer. The first half of the session will be set aside for the speakers. Introduce them and tell the participants there will be a question and answer session following the presentations.

2. After the break, give the participants the option of talking about their genogram progress or their offerings or their reactions to the homework article. Open the discussion on last week's topic and questions.

3. Introduce the research on generational trauma in the Jewish, Armenian, and Native American culture. Distribute the handout of the weekly topic.

4. Assignment: before dismissing, distribute the freewrite questions. Tell the participants that the following articles are recommended additional reading: "Cutting Edge: Christian Imperialism and the Transatlantic Slave Trade" by Katie G. Cannon and "The African American Experience: Forced Immigration and Transgenerational Trauma" by Maurice Apprey.

5. Collect the homework freewrites.

6. Close with prayer.

PART II: LEADER'S GUIDE

LESSON PLAN: SESSION THREE

Generational Trauma in Jewish, Armenian, and Native American History

Objectives

- To meet people who have ministered and received generational healing prayer
- To introduce trauma and generational trauma in other cultures

Note: This schedule assumes a session is from 6:30—8:30 p.m.

Time	Activity	Leader Resources	References and Handouts for Participants
	Turn in freewrite and cinquain		
6:30 (5 min.)	Opening prayer	*Prayers for Dark People*—W. E. B. Dubois	
6:35 (5 min.)	Introduce guest speakers		
6:40 (40 min.)	Guest speakers		
7:20 (10 min.)	Q & A		
7:30 (10 min.)	Break		
7:40 (25 min.)	Class discussions—Genogram check-in; offering		

Generational Trauma

Time	Activity	Leader Resources	References and Handouts for Participants
8:05 (15 min.)	Generational trauma in Jewish, Native American, and Armenian history		Topic handout
8:20	Assignments: Freewrite questions		Freewrite questions
	Closing prayer		

Part II: leader's guide

GENERATIONAL TRAUMA IN JEWISH, ARMENIAN, AND NATIVE AMERICAN HISTORY

Definitions

Trauma—a psychophysical experience of serious threat and/or injury during which frightening thoughts, painful emotions and physical distress occur due to acts of abandonment, aggression, betrayal, stressful events or long-term duress.

Historical trauma—a cumulative emotional and psychological wounding, over lifespans and across generations, emanating from violence inflicted on a large group of people. Historical trauma is an example of how intergenerational pain experienced by an individual in an earlier generation can have effects that reach into the lives of future generations. (Maria Yellow Horse Brave Heart)

Intergenerational Trauma History

Intergenerational trauma was first noticed in 1966 by clinicians who were treating a high number of Canadian clients who were children of survivors of the Holocaust. Dr. Yael Danieli, a practicing clinical psychologist, traumatologist and victimologist, is the co-founder and director of the Group Project for Holocaust Survivors and their Children, and the founding director and former president of the International Society for Traumatic Stress. She is also the editor of the International Handbook of Multigenerational Legacies of Trauma.

Jewish History

The Holocaust was the genocide of approximately six million European Jews during World War II, a program of systematic state-sponsored murder by Nazi Germany, led by Adolf Hitler, throughout Nazi-occupied territory. Some scholars maintain that the definition of the Holocaust should also include Romani, communists, Soviet prisoners of war, Polish and Soviet civilians, homosexuals, people with disabilities, Jehovah's Witnesses and other political and religious opponents who were killed regardless of whether they were German or non-German. Using this definition, the total number of Holocaust victims is between 11 and 17 million.

Most historians claim that the civilian population was unaware of the atrocities that were carried out, especially in the extermination camps, which were located outside of Germany in Nazi-occupied Europe. Significant historical evidence points to the idea that the vast majority of Holocaust victims, prior to their deportation to concentration camps, were unaware of the fate that awaited them. They honestly believed that they were to be resettled.

Motivation for the Holocaust

Antisemitism, Nazi propaganda of a Jewish Communist takeover, racial 'purity'—elimination of the "weaker undesirables."

Method Used in the Holocaust

The persecution and genocide were carried out in stages. Various laws to remove the Jews from civil society, most prominently the Nuremberg Laws, were enacted in Nazi Germany years before the outbreak of World War II. Concentration camps were established in which inmates were subjected to slave labor until they died of exhaustion or disease. Specialized units murdered Jews and political opponents in mass shootings. The occupiers required Jews and Romani to be confined in overcrowded ghettos before being transported by freight train to extermination camps where, if they survived the journey, most were systematically killed in gas chambers.

Manifestation of Trauma

Danieli's studies found the children of Holocaust survivors displayed depression, suicidal ideation and behavior, guilt and concern about betraying the ancestors for being excluded from the suffering, obligation to share in the ancestral pain, a sense of being obliged to take care of and of being responsible for survivor parents, a sense of being obliged to compensate for the genocidal legacy, as well as having grandiose fantasies, dreams, images and perception of the world as dangerous. She named the cluster of characteristics "survivor child complex." In her initial studies, Danieli identified four key concepts:

1) Conspiracy of Silence— survivors were not allowed to talk about their experiences and continued to suffer. This included mental health professionals believing the victims were too emotionally fragile. Silence intensified their profound sense of isolation, loneliness and mistrust of society.

2) Trauma and the Continuity of Self: A Multidimensional, Multidisciplinary Integrative Framework (TCMI)—an individual's identity involves a complex interplay of biology, intrapsychic, familial, social, communal, ethnic, religious, spiritual, educational, economic, legal, political, national, environmental, and international systems. The intensity and duration of the rupture may render the individual vulnerable to further trauma. The Nazi Holocaust ruptured continuity but also destroyed all the individual's existing supports. The conspiracy of silence deprived them and their children of potential agency.

3) Intergenerational Context—Viewed from a family systems perspective, what happened in one generation will affect what happens in the older or younger generation, though the actual behavior may take a variety of forms. Danieli described at least four differing postwar "adaptational styles" of survivor families: Victim families, Fighter families, Numb families, and families of "Those who made it."

4) Vulnerability and/or Resilience—The vulnerability perspective holds that trauma leaves permanent psychic damage that renders survivors more vulnerable when subsequently faced with extreme stress. The resilience perspective holds that coping well with initial trauma will strengthen resistance to the effects of future trauma. Both perspectives recognize individual differences in response to trauma; that exposure to massive trauma may overwhelm predisposition and previous experience, and that post trauma environmental factors play important roles in adaptation.

Coping Strategies

Holocaust survivors and their families retained their history, identity, and culture through their religion. Validation of their identity is nurtured by their faith from within the group. Establishing a homeland in 1948 and renewing their language strengthened their cultural identity. The insistence on commemoration of the event—"never forget." Supporting each other economically, investing in their own communities, gaining economic, political and financial control, and assimilating "in the world but not of it" were additional coping strategies.

Armenian History

Armenia is an ancient nation continually occupying the region of historic Armenia, including what is now northeastern Turkey, from before 500 B.C.E. until their virtual annihilation in 1915. Christianity was brought to Armenia by two of Jesus' disciples, Thaddeus and Bartholomew. Armenia was the first nation to accept Christianity as its state religion in C.E. 301. Conquered by Turkish invaders from the east, Armenia was one of many nations made subject by what was eventually consolidated as the Ottoman Empire. The Turks considered this non-Muslim minority of Armenians as second-class citizens and for centuries subjected them to legal repression. Ottoman imperial expansion led to periods of relative peace and prosperity for the subject populations. But as the empire began to decline, persecutions of all the various minorities increased.

Motivation for the Genocide

The historical situations culminating in the genocide of the Armenians and the destruction of the Jews resemble one another. Both groups were targeted because of their birth membership in a despised group and their religion.

Method Used in the Genocide

A particularly severe series of massacres occurred between 1895 and 1896, when 100,000 to 200,000 Armenians were killed or driven out of the Armenian provinces. The regime removed any possibility of defense or leadership from the Armenian population by disarming and killing all Armenian men in the Turkish army and arresting and killing all current or potential community leaders, including the intelligentsia, religious leaders, merchants and civil servants. The remaining men were then rounded up and killed.

The women, children, and elderly were either forced into slavery or onto death marches; they were frequently attacked by specially organized gangs. They were often held without food for days before the march began, so that they would be too weak to escape, and they were forced to march on the most circuitous, difficult paths to maximize attrition through exhaustion. They were deliberately refused water and had to buy or scrounge for food. Many subsisted on grass. In some areas, Greeks, Jews, and other non-Turkish groups were also forced onto death marches along with the Armenians. Survival rates from the marches were very low. Out of 19,900 Armenians from the three towns of Sivas, Kharput, and Erzerum, only 361 reached the last stop before being driven into the desert, with unknown result. As of 1988, the Armenian presence in Turkey is less than 25,000; reduced from a population of about 2 million. The Turkish government hid the genocide as much as possible, and its successor governments have steadily denied the genocide since, with a disinformation effort that has grown progressively more forceful, sophisticated, and public in recent years.

Manifestations of Trauma

The level of obliterating massive trauma and the deeply personal nature of the persecutors' hatred has made for parallels between the Jewish and Armenians in the reaction of survivors and their families. Symptoms among Armenian survivors that are similar to those of the Jewish Holocaust include anxiety, depression, compulsive associations to trauma-related material, guilt, nightmares, irritability, emptiness, phobias, psychosomatic disorders and severe personality changes, fear of loving and the inability to experience pleasure from activities usually found enjoyable, e.g., hobbies, exercise, sports, social activities. Second generation participants reported manifestations of anxiety in association with extreme parental overprotectiveness. Unique to Armenian survivors is the anger and frustration associated with the denial of the genocide by the Turkish government. They feel alienated and dishonored, their suffering pointless and see the denial as a psychological continuation of the genocide, and a continuing victimization.

Coping Strategies

Several factors historically supported a coherent and persistent sense of Armenian ethnic identity within the Ottoman context. First, the Armenians' ancient origins and the preservation of their historic territory until World War I, gave them a sense of who they were in their own homeland. Second, the Armenian language was distinct from that of surrounding people. Third, the unique Armenian church has remained a central cultural unifying factor for 2000+ years. Fourth is the Millet system of religious self-government within the Ottoman Empire. A study of three generations of several families found a clear commitment to ethnic identity, suggesting the family was able to protect and transmit that identity. All three generations desired to maintain social contact in the Armenian community; to teach their children Armenian history, culture, and traditions, and to give their children Armenian language lessons. The three generations shared a similar perception of the family environment, suggesting that they shared a mutual set of values. There is very strong community cohesion. Each generation in its own way, opposed the intended effects of annihilation and unified the Armenian community to withstand those effects. By existing with an Armenian self-awareness, each family has transmitted this opposition from generation to generation. The active Turkish denial has provided the psychological oppositional pressure that has maintained the effect of a persistent ethnic identity.

Historical Trauma Theory

Dr. Maria Yellow Horse Brave Heart is the president and director/co-founder of the Takini Network of Rapid City, South Dakota and an associate research professor at the University of New Mexico. She has more than twenty years of clinical experience in social work, specifically with the Lakota Nation. She received her MS from the Columbia University School of Social Work and her doctorate from Smith College. Carrying an ancestral legacy of trauma as a lateral descendant of Sitting Bull, and a member of the White Lance extended family kinship network who are Wounded Knee descendants, Maria Yellow Horse Brave Heart became conscious of her own unresolved historical trauma in 1978. In 1988, she developed the theoretical construct of the historical trauma response. Dr. Brave Heart is also a member of the International Society for Traumatic Stress Studies.

Part II: leader's guide

Lakota Native American History

In 1890, Sitting Bull, the personification of traditional Lakota leadership and resistance, was viewed as a threat by US government officials. On December 15, 1890, Sitting Bull was assassinated. Several of his survivors and followers fled in fear to join Bigfoot. Bigfoot and his band also feared persecution by the cavalry who in fact followed them to Wounded Knee. There, these hundreds of Lakota were disarmed and then massacred at Wounded Knee Creek on December 29,1890; their bodies thrown into a mass grave. An additional trauma for Native people has been the placement of American Indian children in the boarding schools, sometimes over 1,000 miles away from families and tribal communities, under federal policy since 1879. Studies describe Native children being shackled and chained to bedposts, and beaten in boarding schools. Further, overcrowded and deficient conditions fueled the tuberculosis epidemic from which more than one-third of the Lakota population over one year of age died between 1936 and 1941. Gradually, many boarding schools were replaced with regular reservation day schools, but individuals report boarding school trauma even as late as the 1970s.

Motivation for the Massacre

The occupation of land and the dislike of a people with a different culture and religious beliefs by Europeans and European Americans.

Manifestation of the Trauma

Manifestations of the historical trauma response include depression, self-destructive behavior, psychic numbing, poor affect tolerance, anger, and elevated mortality rates from suicide and cardiovascular diseases were observed among Jewish Holocaust survivors and descendants, as well as among the Lakota. Lakota mortality rates for heart disease are almost two times the rate for the general United States population; suicide rates are more than twice the national average. The association of heart disease with PTSD and other psychiatric conditions such as depression has been identified. Current lifespan trauma, superimposed upon a traumatic ancestral past, creates additional challenges for Lakota survivors. The pervasiveness and frequency of chronic traumatic exposure among modern American Indian youth has been recognized.

Coping Strategies

In 1992 Brave Heart co-founded The Takini Network, a collective of traditional Lakota and other Native service providers and community leaders, dedicated to helping Native communities heal from historical traumas . The programs incorporate Lakota history with a focus on the commonality among the Lakota of shared trauma and emphasize traditional Lakota spirituality and values and practices of generosity, deep emotional attachments, loyalty, hard work and service to others.

Similarities and Differences

Survivor guilt is a major manifestation of survivor syndrome among Jewish Holocaust survivors. A comparison of Armenian and Jewish literary responses to these two genocides noted that the sense of remorseful guilt in some Jewish writings is largely absent from Armenian literature. The respondents' guilt was associated with duties to the living (i.e., not having done enough for the Armenian community) and among the second generation, not having done enough for their survivor parents. The commemorative function of guilt may not be as imperative or culturally supported among Armenians on a personal level because of their Christian belief in the afterlife. The psychological function of commemoration may be adequately served on a community level by the church service of commemoration for the genocide victims. Also, Turkey's active, ongoing denial of their victimization may have created an abiding anger that overshadows any experience of guilt for surviving and prospering. Another factor that differs between the two groups is that the "conspiracy of silence" found in the Jewish community was internal between the survivors and those who did not experience it. The silence left the Holocaust survivors profoundly rebuffed, alienated, and mistrustful. The "conspiracy of silence" for the Armenians was different because it came from outside the community. The silence did not create a chasm within the Armenian community because the genocide had affected virtually all Armenians.

Part II: Leader's Guide

The Lakota historical trauma response is analogous to the survivor syndrome and survivor's child complex identified among those who endured the Jewish Holocaust, and their descendants and similar traits in other trauma survivors and descendants. Specific features of this historical trauma response include (a) transposition of where one lives simultaneously in the past and the present with the ancestral suffering as the main organizing principal in one's life; (b) identification with the dead so that one feels psychically (emotionally and psychologically) dead and feels unworthy of living; and (c) maintaining loyalty to and identification with the suffering of deceased ancestors, re-enacting affliction within one's own life. Additionally, there is survivor guilt, an ensuing fixation to trauma, reparatory fantasies, and attempts to undo the tragedy of the past.

FREEWRITE HOMEWORK QUESTIONS

Session Three: Generational Trauma in Jewish, Armenian and Native American History

Session Questions

The first question was the question you started in class. You can complete it or choose another question. You can answer all three if you choose. Make two copies of your freewrite, one to turn in and one to contribute to the class discussion.

1) What was an 'aha' moment for you as we discussed trauma? What did it mean to you?

2) Was there information about the Jewish Holocaust, the Armenian Genocide or Native American Massacres that promoted a better understanding of generational trauma? If yes, what? If no, why?

3) In response to the definitions of trauma and historical trauma, what types of threat or injury can you identify in these events?

First additional reading: Apprey, Maurice. "The African American Experience: Forced Immigration and Transgenerational Trauma." *Mind and Human Interaction* (1993): 70–75

Second additional reading: Cannon, Katie Geneva. "Cutting Edge Christian Imperialism and the Transatlantic Slave Trade." *Journal of Feminist Studies*. Indiana Press (2008):127–134.

Pick and answer at least one statement. You can answer all three if you choose. Make two copies of your freewrite, one to turn in and one to contribute to the class discussion.

1) My thoughts after reading these articles are . . .

2) Having read these articles, I would like to know more about . . .

3) Questions that came to mind as I read these articles were . . .

Don't forget to bring your weekly offering!!!!!

ROOTS MATTER: HEALING HISTORY,
HONORING HERITAGE, RENEWING HOPE

Session Four

Generational Trauma in African American History

Generational Trauma in African American History

SESSION FOUR

Introduction

The focus of this session is the generational trauma in African American history. Because of the personal nature of the homework material, be aware of the mood of the class. By this time the format of the class will be familiar and the level of intimacy will deepen.

Objectives

The two objectives for this session are:

- To identify trauma types and traumatic events in African American history
- To compare similarities and differences among Jewish, Armenian and Native American generational trauma

Preparation

- A copy of *Prayers for Dark People* by W.E.B. Dubois or other devotional material for the opening prayer
- *Africans in America* DVD chapter 6 "Let Him Return" Olaudah Equiano
- Offering
- Topic handout
- Trauma definitions (see Appendix C.)
- Homework freewrite questions

Session Outline

1. As part of the devotional exercise and after the opening prayer, have the participants watch chapter 6 of *Africans in America*. Direct them to write a cinquain on what they watched. Close the devotional exercise by having the participants read their cinquains. End each reading with the phrase "ashe (ah- shay)—let it be so."

Part II: Leader's Guide

2. Have the participants report about progress with their genogram—questions, insights, experiences, obstacles.

3. Open the discussion about last week's topic and questions.

4. After the break, have the participants share their offerings for the week. Ask each to pass it around to the rest of the group after sharing his/her story.

5. Introduce the research done on African American generational trauma. Distribute the handout of the weekly topic and trauma definitions.

6. Assignment: before dismissing, distribute the freewrite questions. Tell the participants that the following articles are recommended additional reading: "The Middle Passage, Trauma and the Tragic Re-Imagination of African American Theology" by Matthew Johnson and "Racism and Economics: The Perspective of Oliver Cox" by Katie G. Cannon.

7. Collect the homework freewrites.

8. Close with prayer.

LESSON PLAN: SESSION FOUR

Generational Trauma in African American History

Objectives

- To identify types and trauma events in African American history
- To compare Jewish, Armenian, and Native American trauma events

Note: This schedule assumes a session is from 6:30—8:30 p.m.

Time	Activity	Leader Resources	References and Handouts for Participants
	Turn in freewrite and cinquain		
6:30 (10 min.)	Opening prayer Video clip	DVD *Africans in America* chapter 6 "Let Him Return" Olaudah Equiano	
6:40 (10 min.)	Cinquain devotional		
6:50 (10 min.)	Genogram check-in; experiences, insights, obstacles, etc.		
7:00 (30 min.)	Conversations on freewrite on session		
7:30 (10 min.)	Break		
7:40 (20 min.)	Offerings		
8:00 (25 min.)	Trauma types Generational trauma in African American history		Topic handout Trauma definitions

Part II: Leader's Guide

Time	Activity	Leader Resources	References and Handouts for Participants
8:25	Assignments Freewrite questions		Freewrite questions
	Closing prayer		

GENERATIONAL TRAUMA IN AFRICAN AMERICAN HISTORY

History

Ron Eyerman

- Slavery is a cultural marker in the formation of African American identity.
- Slavery is a site of memory requiring constant reflection and reinterpretation.
- Slavery is an historic event present in every African American's consciousness.
- Different generations have different perspectives because of time and circumstances.
- All generations need to interpret and come to terms with their collective trauma.

Elaine Pinderhughes

- African Americans were the only group whose immigration was forced and brutal.
- African Americans were the only group whose subsequent existence was determined by legalized inequality.
- These conditions exert ongoing and unrelenting disruptive effects on their efforts to build cohesive families and communities to ensure their survival.

David Eltis and David Richardson

- From 1501—1867, an estimated 12.5 million Africans were forcibly displaced by the transatlantic slave trade.
- Of the 12.5 million, an estimated 10.7 million arrived in North and South America and the Caribbean.
- Initially, the Europeans had no master plan for slavery.

- The first African slaves arrived from Europe, not Africa, in the early 1500s.
- The first slave ship sailed directly from Africa to Northern Brazil in 1520.
- Initially, Amerindians were the source of labor on the sugar plantations.
- Brazil and the Caribbean received 90 percent of all enslaved Africans. The countries were: Senegambia, 6 percent; Sierra Leone, 3.1 percent; the Windward Coast, 2.7 percent; the Gold Coast, 9.7 percent; Bight of Benin, 16 percent; Bight of Biafra, 12.7 percent; West Central Africa (Congo), 45 percent; St. Helena, southeast Africa and the Indian Ocean Islands (Mozambique), 4.3 percent.
- During the Middle Passage: 26 percent were children; 12–13 percent did not survive; the average trip was two months.
- The human misery quotient of the middle passage is unmatched.

These statistics illustrate the atrocious magnitude, longevity and diversity of trauma experienced by the Africans brought to the Americas and the Caribbean. The trauma is deeply rooted in the spirit, psyche and memory of the people.

Motivation—Economics

The total dollar value of slaves held in the South, expressed in historical dollars and adjusted for inflation, generally represented a full one third or more of all liquid capital in the entire South. The normal expected rate of return on slave investments was roughly 10 percent. By 1850, future profits based on prices relative to rentals predicted that gains by the 1860's would be bigger than ever in the slave-trading business.

Cotton was the consummate partnership between southern agriculture and northern industrial processes and mill production, and the largest US export. Richmond, the slave center of the US sold, bought and hired as many as 10,000 slaves per month. On the eve of the Civil War, the slave trade had more economic impact on the US national economy than any other single type of industry.

Slaves were the single largest financial asset in the US, worth over $3.5 billion in 1860 dollars (97.65 billion in today's dollars)—more than the value of America's railroads, banks, factories or ships. In 1858, Templeton and Goodwin's auction business in Richmond earned nearly $3 million in gross sales in 2011 dollars. Hector Davis reported $1.7 million in 1858, which would be more than $68 million in 2011 dollars. Slaves were insured. George was insured by Joseph Myers in 1858 in Richmond (Henrico County) for a five year period for a $19.40 premium. If George died, Myers would receive a $1000 payout.

In the 1860 census, 26 percent of all Southern families owned slaves, many on a speculative basis as an investment or as a hedge against economic turbulence. In Virginia, the percentage of slave-owning families was 26 percent. In 1860 the South had 60 of the nation's most wealthy men, in spite of having less than one-third of the free population. The average per capita income in the south was $3,978 in comparison with $2,040 in the North.

On the typical plantation with twenty slaves, the slaves themselves (or their hired labor value) were worth more than the total value of the land and implements combined. Slaves become more of a currency than the dollar and served as an investment and a hedge against inflation and economic hard times. One can argue that just as the US later utilized a currency pegged to the gold standard, the antebellum South utilized a currency pegged to the chattel standard.

Methods Used

- forced cutting off of Africans from their cultural roots and deliberate separation of people who shared tribal connections,
- massive disruption of previous cultural traditions,
- cruel and inhuman slave practices that promoted a view of slaves as chattel actively undermined marriage,
- broke up families through slave sales,
- actively undermined men's role as protector and provider for their families,
- sexually abused women and used them as breeders,

Part II: leader's guide

- demanded obedience and absolute control, including overall communication,
- legally prohibited education,
- forced slaves to be dependent, submissive, fearful of their masters,
- forced slaves to regard themselves as inferior.

Manifestation of Trauma

These realities are the endpoint of centuries of accumulated loss, traumatization and transmission of racial stress.

- the high rate of poverty
- marital disruption
- single-parent families
- incarceration
- drug and alcohol abuse
- homelessness
- poor school achievement and dropout
- children in foster care
- disparities in health morbidity and mortality

Joy DeGruy Leary

Multigenerational trauma, together with continued oppression and absence of opportunity to access the benefits available in the society leads to Post Traumatic Slave Syndrome (PTSS).

Post Traumatic Slave Syndrome—a condition that exists when a population has experienced multigenerational trauma resulting from:

- centuries of slavery
- continued experience of oppression
- institutionalized racism
- belief (real or imagined) that the benefits of the society in which they live are not accessible to them

PTSS is a syndrome, a pattern of behaviors that is brought about by specific circumstances. DeGruy defines three categories of behavior:

Vacant Esteem is the state of believing oneself to have little or no worth, exacerbated by the group and societal pronouncement of inferiority.

- three spheres of influence : society, community and family
- signs of vacant esteem: despair, fear of living
- undermining achievements of other African Americans
- difficulty in celebrating the success of others. (The belief that one has little or no value produces behaviors that almost demand the devaluing of others.)

Ever Present Anger—In its simplest form, anger is the normal emotional response to a blocked goal. It is a response to the failure of America to successfully integrate its black citizenry into the social and political fabric of America, to allow them fair and equal access.

- Slavery was an inherently angry and violent process. White people molded anger and violence in every aspect of enslavement.
- Any group of people living under such harsh conditions would eventually learn the ways of their captors.

Racist Socialization (self-hate) is the adoption of the slave master's value system that white and all things associated with whiteness are superior; and that black, and all things associated with blackness, are inferior, e.g., standards of beauty (skin color and hair).

- giving into stereotypes, e.g., glamorizing thug life, sexual promiscuity, lack of education, electing sports and entertainment as primary avenues of achievement
- slave owners perpetuated feelings of separateness and distrust by ordering some black slaves to beat or otherwise punish their friends, peers and relatives
- Black overseers were often more brutal than their white counterparts for two reasons: 1) they did not want to be perceived as being lenient

and so lose their position, and 2) the slave masters rewarded them for their cruelty.

Coping Strategies

- adapting the Christian message
- worship
- spirituality
- music
- family & extended family
- running away
- breaking tools
- work slow down
- psychological mind games
- learning to read

After emancipation, church membership, social organizations, social events, e.g., homecoming, reunions, parties, dances, church programs, sports, work, extended family, fictive kinship, literacy, education, entrepreneurial endeavors, were ways in which African Americans created a new culture for themselves. Drugs, alcohol and domestic violence, physical and sexual abuse were (and still are) some of the destructive coping strategies.

FREEWRITE HOMEWORK QUESTIONS

Session Four—Generational Trauma in African American History

Session Questions

The first question was the question you started in class. You can complete it or choose another question. You can answer all three if you choose. Make two copies of your freewrite, one to turn in and one to contribute to the class discussion.

1) What have you learned about your family history that has given you a new understanding of trauma in your family?

2) Do you see evidence of trauma in your family? What kind? In what way did it affect the family? Has it influenced you? If so, how?

3) Can you identify patterns of behavior, illness, or episodes in your family that started with a traumatic event?

Additional reading: Johnson, Matthew "The Middle Passage, Trauma and the Tragic Re-Imagination of African American Theology." *Pastoral Psychology* 53, no. 6 (July 2005): 541–61.

Pick and answer at least one statement. You can answer all three if you choose. Make two copies of your freewrite, one to turn in and one to contribute to the class discussion.

1) My thoughts after reading this article are . . .

2) Having read this article, I would like to know more about . . .

3) Questions that came to mind as I read this article were . . .

Don't forget to bring your weekly offering!!!!!

ROOTS MATTER: HEALING HISTORY,
HONORING HERITAGE, RENEWING HOPE

Session Five

Trauma, Mourning, Resilience, and Hope

Trauma, Mourning, Resilience, and Hope

SESSION FIVE

Introduction

This is the last session in which new materials will be introduced, so be aware of any loose ends that need to be addressed. Any special preparation or requirements for the healing service needed to be announced. Make sure the participants understand the importance of completing the evaluation form.

Objectives

The two objectives for this session are:

- To identify the resilience, resistance and hope in the African American religious tradition
- To explain the format of the healing service

Preparation

- A copy of *Prayers for Dark People* by W. E. B. Dubois or other devotional material for the opening prayer
- *Unchained Memories* DVD Time: 38:01–46:15 (Sam Jackson—paddy rollers)
- Offering
- Topic handout
- Homework freewrite questions
- Homework lament assignment
- Evaluation form (See Appendix D.)

Session Outline

1. As part of the devotional exercise and after the opening prayer, have the participants watch the video clip from *Unchained Memories*. Direct them to write a cinquain on what they watched. Close the devotional

Part II: Leader's Guide

exercise by having the participants read their cinquains. End each reading with the phrase "ashe (ah -shay)—let it be so."

2. Have the participants report about their progress with their genogram—questions, insights, experiences, obstacles.
3. Open the discussion about last week's topic and questions.
4. After the break, have the participants share their offerings for the week. Have them pass it around to the rest of the class after sharing their story.
5. Introduce the topic on the theological and spiritual impact of major trauma. Distribute the handout of the weekly topic.
6. Remind the participants to complete their evaluations and that the first hour of session will be to discuss the evaluation and recommendations. The second hour will be the healing service.
7. Assignment: Before dismissing, distribute the freewrite questions, the instructions on writing a lament for the healing service, and the evaluation forms.
8. Collect the homework freewrites.
9. Close with prayer.

LESSON PLAN: SESSION FIVE

Trauma, Mourning, Resilience, and Hope

Objective

- To identify strengths and resilience in the African American religious tradition

Note: this schedule assumes the session is from 6:30—8:30 p.m.

Time	Activity	Leader Resources	References and Handouts for Participants
	Turn in freewrite and cinquain		
6:30 (10 min.)	Opening prayer Video clip	DVD *Unchained Memories* Sam Jackson—time count 38:01—46:15	
6:40 (10 min.)	Cinquain devotional		
6:50 (10 min.)	Genogram check-in; experiences, insights, obstacles, etc.	Set date for follow-up meeting in four months	
7:00 (30 min.)	Conversations on freewrite		
7:30 (10 min.)	Break		
7:40 (20 min.)	Offerings		
8:00 (25 min.)	African American religious tradition	Fact sheets and trauma sheets	Topic handout
	Discuss Healing Service		

Part II: Leader's Guide

Time	Activity	Leader Resources	References and Handouts for Participants
8:25	Assignments: freewrite questions; lament		Freewrite questions Lament instructions
	Closing prayer		

TRAUMA, MOURNING, RESILIENCE, HOPE

Theological and Spiritual Impact of Major Trauma

Crisis of Faith—Some people find a new, different or stronger faith as a result of trauma; others lose their faith. Everyone who is traumatized must at least pause and re-examine his/her theological assumptions. Some spiritual work is an inevitable part of the healing process.

Crisis of Meaning—Where we find meaning and purpose in life might be called into question by a trauma. It takes the forms of questions: Why did I survive? Why have you kept going? Trauma is often a meaningless event.

Shattered Assumptions—Trauma leads to at least a temporary shattering of one's basic assumptions about life, self, the world, and other people. Janoff-Bulman in *Shattered Assumptions* cites three assumptions that are typically shattered: "Life is fair, People are generally good and Life is good and predictable."

David Richo in *The Five Things We Cannot Change..and the Happiness We Find by Embracing Them* states that there are five "unavoidable givens" in life that cannot be controlled or changed. The unavoidable givens are: Everything changes and ends; Things do not go according to plan; Life is not always fair; Pain is part of life; and People are not loving and loyal all the time.

Kent Drescher, a clinician who specializes in military veterans and coauthor of *An Exploration of Viability and Usefulness of the Construct of Moral Injury in War Veterans* uses "moral injury" to describe the spiritual issue in PTSD. Veterans have lost faith in humanity, and a sense of right and wrong.

Why are intentional human traumas more difficult to deal with than accidental traumas or natural disasters? Does not the former shatter our assumptions about the good nature of humanity?

Violation or disruption of basic trust—Erik Erikson argued that the basic trust that life is predictable and good is set early in life, and forms the "cornerstone of the healthy personality." Trauma disrupts basic trust or faith.

Forgiveness—Why should I? and If so, how? are questions raised by trauma. Forgiving others for their actions or reactions, forgiving self for actions or reactions, forgiving God for action or inaction.

Changes in the image of God—Studies document how one's image of God changes in the course of trauma. Theodicy questions: Is God all powerful? Is God loving? Does evil exist? The image may change to a more unpredictable, random and cold God, or a more merciful image of God as one who comes close to comfort. Some may come to see God as gentler. Some may come to see evil as really only temporary.

Evil—People who have experienced great trauma and abuse often have a new and deeper appreciation of evil.

Every loss involves a radicalization of values, priorities. People become less materialistic, more relationship oriented. Trauma forces us to realize our dependency on God. Whenever we suffer, we must rely on others and God to get by. We must challenge our own self-reliance and self-sufficiency.

Mourning

Vamik Volkan observes "When a whole society has undergone massive trauma, victimized adults may endure guilt and shame for not having protected their children. The by-product of such trauma is a perennial, collective mourning over the loss of group dignity, self-esteem and identity. The mourning is characterized by conscious and unconscious communications passed down to generations in an attempt to mourn the group's losses and remove the collective sense of victimization . . . If a sense of relief is to be found, the mourning related to the losses and trauma must be worked through, and the humiliation must be reversed."

The mourning process is the letting go process, making the adjustment to the loss. Grief is part of mourning; it is the pain of the loss. Mourning is the adjustment to the loss. How does one do that? How does one work through the losses, trauma and humiliation, the feelings of powerlessness?

As we have seen in other cultures, silence is a formidable deterrent to mourning—acknowledging the loss and the trauma. Shame, humiliation, anger, fear, helplessness can stifle the mourning. We are encouraged to forget, just get on with it. When trauma is "swept under the rug" it goes underground; it becomes internal and unconscious. Spirituality and religion connect with the internal and the unconscious. It plays an important part in maintaining community, identity and culture.

Resilience

Resilience is the ability to adapt to difficult or challenging life experiences wherein a person overcomes adversity, recovers from disruptive change or misfortune in order to thrive under extreme, on-going pressure without acting in dysfunctional or harmful ways. In *Soul Theology*, Harold Carter identifies the core beliefs African Americans have about God and themselves as a Christian community. These are the beliefs that have been passed down and maintained by generations. This is where resilience is formed and sustained. This is where hope is "kept alive."

Core Beliefs about God

God is in charge—"life looks pretty bad at times, but I have learned that when one door is slammed shut, God reserves the right to open a larger one for me."

God is a just God—the belief that no oppression goes unpunished and no sacrificial suffering goes unnoticed and unrewarded. What goes around comes around.

God is a mighty God—God's power works in living history. Songs such as "Leaning on the Everlasting Arms," "Peace Be Still," scripture quotes such as "Is there anything too hard for the Lord" or "He that dwells in the secret places of the most high shall abide under the shadow of the Almighty" affirm belief in God being a mighty God.

God is an all knowing God—The God of the universe must know when and how to exercise God's might to relieve stressful situations and keep life within bearable bounds. The slaves used to sing "My God is writing all the time. . .he see all you do, an' he hears all you say, my God is writing all the time."

God is a good God—All that God makes is good. There is evil in the world; "weeping endures for the night, but joy comes in the morning." "I'm so glad trouble don't last always." "Earth has no sorrow that heaven cannot heal."

God is a gracious God—No wrongdoing (sin) renders one unacceptable if one takes responsibility for the wrongdoing (confession) and commits to changing one's attitude, behavior, etc. (repentance). There is a balm in Gilead to make the wounded whole . . . to heal the sin-sick soul.

Core Beliefs about Self

We are all equal in God's sight—not identical, equal. "There is neither Jew or Gentile, bond or free, male or female . . . we are all one in Christ Jesus."

We are all unique and worthy of respect. The scripture says "Stir up the gift of God which is in you." The song says "This little light of mine, I'm gonna let it shine."

We all belong to the family of God. The Akan and Ashanti proverb says "Because we are, I am." We extend our family beyond the bloodline calling ourselves aunt and uncle, cousin, second mother, spiritual father. In church we are brothers and sisters in Christ. It is preached that we bear each other's burdens and in as much as we do for the least of these we do for Christ.

We can persevere and endure. We don't have to surrender to the pressures of life and give up in despair. The test of our faith is its ability to sustain and empower people and help them cope with life. "Those that wait on the Lord will renew their strength" . . . "On Christ the solid rock I stand all other ground is sinking sand."

Hope

Hope is the expectation, anticipation, wish, longing for, dreaming of justice, equality, fairness in order to create wholeness, freedom, healing, peace, and well-being. It takes courage to move into the inner pain of loss or trauma.

Trauma, Mourning, Resilience, and Hope

Hope is belief that in spite of the pain, it will be better on the other side and that healing is found by going through it.

Do/did we, as a people collectively or individually intentionally mourn the losses of our ancestors, our families, ourselves? Is it our music? Do/did we mourn through our music, through our sorrow songs, the spirituals, gospels and contemporary gospel, blues, jazz, rhythm and blues, protest songs, hip-hop, rap? If we didn't sing would we be here?

Do/did know we are mourning when we sing? Do/did we know we are hoping when we sing? Does the African American resilience come from our ability to mourn and hope? What other ways did/do we hope? What other ways were/are we resilient? What other ways did/do we mourn? What other ways did/do we deal with trauma?

PART II: LEADER'S GUIDE

FREEWRITE HOMEWORK QUESTIONS

Session Six—The African American Religious Tradition of Resilience and Hope

Session Questions

The first question was the question you started in class. You can complete it or choose another question. Answer at least three questions. You can answer all of them if you choose. Make two copies of your freewrite, one to turn in and one to contribute to the class discussion.

1) What were the practices or beliefs your family used to sustain their faith/religion/spirituality? How have they influenced you?

2) What were the most effective ways you have experienced prayer for yourself, your family and your community?

3) What are some of the gifts, talents, special skills, and examples of resilience in your family? Is there evidence that they have been passed down? What kind? In what way did they affect the family? Have they influenced you? If so, how?

4) Other than the intercessory prayers in the healing stories in scripture, can you describe stories of healing by intercessory prayer in your life or in the life of someone you know? How was the healing revealed? Physically? Emotionally? Relationally?

5) What were some of the ways in which the African American church created a religion/faith that sustained them? How did they accomplish that? What were some of the beliefs that the ancestors held on to? Why do you think they were important?

Don't forget to bring your offerings!!!!!

Lament Assignment

The lament is a ritual expression for the feelings of being sinned against. It asks the question "My God, My God why have you forsaken me/us?" Reflect on the generational trauma you have read about, thought about, written about or listened to in this class—large or small, shocking or subtle, current or past. Reconnect with those feelings, thoughts and reactions. In the format of a lamentation, write a poetic one page lament, a complaint or plea addressed to God. Be honest and raw. Let the rage out. You can edit it to contribute to the healing service; you can write a second one for public consumption; it can be for your eyes only. The important thing is to be honest. You may want to read the book of Lamentations. Below is an excerpt from Kathleen O'Connor, *Jeremiah: Pain and Promise*, chapter 8: Survive by Praying: The Confessions, pp. 89–90.

> Perhaps it is the capacity of laments to bring unspeakable suffering into the light that expands the heart and makes room for hope to emerge across the gap of emptiness . . . Jeremiah's prayers make him a model for other sufferers, an ideal survivor. His words honor suffering in its many bitter dimensions and give voice to the mute pain of destroyed faith. They reflect back to victims their own spiritual and theological quagmire . . . Here is what to do in the pit of hopelessness: cling to God, even when God has slipped away. Yell at the top of your collective lungs. Hold tightly, mercilessly, and with every ounce of strength, shout and scream at the deity. Tell the truth, voice the rage and despair right to the face of the "Just Judge." Hold nothing back. Complain, protest, resist. Reclaim experience of misery and pain, see them and name them before God. "Give God an account" and approach God "like a prince" to return to the words of that other God resister (Job 31:37). Communicate all that is shattered, despair-creating, and spirit-defeating. Lay it out so you can see yourselves and can see each other in this deep, unending wound. God is hidden there in that space . . . Turning to the disappeared God is how to survive disaster. Public, communal worship can revivify life with the God of their past. Jeremiah's confessions give shape and words with which to do this by reinvention, retrieving and retooling traditional liturgical prayers of lament . . . It is exactly the lament's bitter assaults on divine justice that paradoxically make them into a perfect vehicle of fidelity.

ROOTS MATTER: HEALING HISTORY,
HONORING HERITAGE, RENEWING HOPE

Session Six

Evaluation and Healing Service

EVALUATION AND HEALING SERVICE

SESSION SIX

Introduction

This is the final session and culmination of the program. Make sure there is opportunity for closure with this session. Offer any follow-up assistance if needed. It may be helpful to set a date to meet and see how everyone is doing.

Objectives

The two objectives of this session are:

- To obtain feedback from the participants about the effectiveness of the program
- To offer opportunity for the participants to pray for generational healing of their families

Preparation

- A copy of *Prayers for Dark People* by W. E. B. Dubois or other devotional material for the opening prayer
- Decorations for table, communion dishes and elements
- Music for service
- Evaluation form (See Appendix D.)
- Healing service program (See Appendix E.)
- Program certificates and mementos
- Camera

Session Outline

1. Begin the session with an opening prayer. Invite the participants to eat during this part of the session, if they had not eaten earlier.
2. Lead the participants in the evaluation of the program. Make extra copies of the evaluation forms available for those who have not

PART II: LEADER'S GUIDE

completed one. Ask for suggestions for improvement, as well as the names of any groups or audiences that might be interested.

3. After the break, distribute the healing service programs.
4. End with a benediction.

EVALUATION AND HEALING SERVICE

LESSON PLAN: SESSION SIX

Evaluation and Healing Service

Objectives

- To obtain feedback from the participants about the effectiveness of the program
- To offer opportunity for the participants to pray for generational healing of their families

Note: this schedule assumes the session will be from 6:30—8:30 p.m.

Time	Activity	Leader Resources	References and Handouts for Participants
		Decorations for table, communion elements and dishes, music	
6:30 (5 min.)	Opening prayer	*Prayers for Dark People* W. E. B. Dubois	
6:35 (55 min.)	Reflections and evaluations		Evaluation forms
7:30 (10 min.)	Break		
7:40 (50 min.)	Healing Service		Healing Service programs
8:30	Closing prayer		Program mementos

ROOTS MATTER: HEALING HISTORY,
HONORING HERITAGE, RENEWING HOPE

Session Seven

Follow-up Session (optional)

Follow-up Session (optional)

SESSION SEVEN

Introduction

This is the follow-up session which was scheduled during session five. This is an optional session. If this session is held, make sure there is opportunity for continued connection and assistance.

Objective

The objective for this session is:

- To obtain feedback from participants about the long term effectiveness of their program participation on them and their families

Preparation

- Email follow-up questions two weeks before the session.
- A copy of *Conversations with God* by James Washington or other devotional material for the opening prayer
- Make extra copies of follow-up questions available for those who have not completed them.

Session Outline

1. Begin the session with an opening prayer. Invite the participants to eat during this part of the session.
2. Lead the participants in the conversation about how their participation in the course has influenced them and/or their family members by identifying significant events, sensitivity or awareness, etc.
3. End with a benediction.
4. Take a group picture.

PART II: LEADER'S GUIDE

LESSON PLAN: SESSION SEVEN

Follow-up Session (optional)

Objectives

- To obtain feedback from participants about the effectiveness of the course
- To offer opportunity for participants to pray for generational healing of their families

Note: this schedule assumes the session is from 6:30—8:30 p.m.

Time	Activity	Leader Resources	References and Handouts for Participants
6:30 (5 min.)	Opening prayer	*Conversations with God* James Washington	
6:35 (55 min.)	Reflections		Follow-up questions
7:30 (10 min.)	Break		
7:40 (35 min.)	Reflections		
8:15 (15 min.)	Have participants answer three of the follow-up questions and collect them		
8:30	Closing prayer		
	Group picture	camera	

FOLLOW-UP SESSION (OPTIONAL)

FOLLOW-UP QUESTIONS

1. Can you describe an image to describe your experience in the program?
2. What was your experience of the healing service?
3. Since completing the course have you discovered practices, values or beliefs that fostered resilience and resistance in your family to sustain the challenges of life? If so, what were some of them?
4. Were there any "aha" moments for you as a result of being in the program? What were they? What did they mean to you?
5. As a result of the course, did you have a better understanding of trauma or generational trauma? If yes, what? If no, why?
6. What have you learned from this program that gave you a new understanding of your family history?
7. Have relationships with your family members changed since the session? If yes, how? If no, why not?
8. Have you done anything differently with your family members since the end of the program? If yes, what? If no, why not?

Illustration

Table 1: Class Project Expenses September 4—October 9, 2012

Items	Sept 4	Sept 11	Sept 18	Sept 25	Oct 2, 2012	Oct 9, 2012	Total
Binders	$58.00						$58.00
Dividers	$21.00						$21.00
Templates	$111.09						111.09
Colored Paper	$8.56					$10.13	$18.69
Note Paper	$3.15						$3.15
Books	$256.00						$256.00
Articles	$127.22						$127.22
Handouts	$10.40	$3.15	$12.76	$14.39	$8.19	$10.80	$59.69
Music						$24.96	$24.96
Africans In America DVD	$59.99						$59.99
Unchained Memories DVD	$35.09						$35.09
Food	$65.00	$65.00	$65.00	$65.00	$65.00	$65.00	$390.00
Staff	$85.00	$85.00	$85.00	$85.00	$85.00	$85.00	$510.00

ILLUSTRATION

Items	Sept 4	Sept 11	Sept 18	Sept 25	Oct 2, 2012	Oct 9, 2012	Total
Paper Products	$125.00						$125.00
Childcare							
Classroom							
Storage Boxes	$10.49						$10.49
Gas	$5.75	$5.75	$5.75	$5.75	$5.75	$5.75	$34.50
Communion Supplies						$19.95	$19.95
Certificates						$10.49	$10.49
Ribbon						$3.14	$3.14
Gift card for 2 speakers			$50.00				$50.00
Tent Cards & Sharpie	$18.14						$18.14
Total	$999.88	$158.90	$218.51	$170.14	$163.94	$235.22	1946.59

Appendix A
Consent Form

Introduction/Purpose

The effects of generational trauma have been identified and studied in the Jewish, Native American, Armenian and African American communities. Literature on the Jewish Holocaust, Native American Massacres, Armenian Genocide and the African American Slave Trade describes the intergenerational transmission of trauma, grief, and loss. Healthcare professionals, social scientists, historians, and theologians have identified economic, social, religious, cultural and educational patterns of behavior that are processes perpetuated from generation to generation. By using the genogram, the inherited positive and negative patterns and their effects on the lives of the individuals, families and communities can be understood.

You are being asked to participate in a program that is focused on transgenerational trauma in the African American community and that identifies biblical themes and theological concepts of forgiveness, suffering, *imago Dei* (image of God) and healing.

You are being asked to participate in this program because you are a member of the African American community. We are interested in the opinions of adults about this topic; and, you are part of the Christian church community from which this project is seeking information.

Appendix A

The purpose of this program is to:

- identify patterns of historical trauma in family members that were inherited from African ancestors who experienced chattel slavery;
- recognize the resilience, coping mechanisms, and strength inherited from previous generations in your families;
- discern the biblical, psychosocial, and spiritual connections;
- use the genogram as a tool for intercessory prayer;
- write an intercessory prayer;
- discuss aspects of a healing ritual framework that remembers the ancestors, honors current family members and releases hope for the future generations.

There will be ten to sixteen persons participating in this program.

The potential benefits to you from participating in this program may include:

- a greater awareness of the effects of transgenerational trauma on the family;
- the importance of forgiveness in the healing process;
- the important part faith plays in the resiliency of family members;
- a new way to approach intercessory prayer for family;
- the importance of knowing family and cultural/ethnic history.

Your participation in this program may aid in understanding:

- how these sessions can help other families find ways to heal themselves and their families through generational healing prayer;
- how healing is manifested in families.

As a participant, you will be expected to attend all six sessions:

Dates: [enter the dates of the program]
Time: [enter the time of the program]
Location: [enter the location where the program will be held]

Consent Form

Each session will build on the previous one, therefore you are asked to make an earnest commitment to attend all six sessions. Your participation in this program may be discontinued without your consent if you miss any two of the first three sessions.

You are asked to arrive thirty minutes prior to the start of a session. Light refreshments will be provided. The session will begin promptly at 6:30 pm.

You will be introduced to some form of reflection.

You will be asked to:
- freewrite in response to the reflection;
- verbally respond to the opening reflection;
- create a genogram of your family;
- participate in session activities;
- participate in a generational healing service;
- complete assigned readings and homework;
- complete a course evaluation form;
- participate in a follow-up group or individual meeting within four months.

Your participation in this program may involve risks.
- You may feel emotionally or physically overwhelmed by the material presented.
- You may feel emotionally or physically upset when doing the assigned activities or readings.
- Some of the material studied and discussed may cause emotional discomfort due to the graphic and violent nature of the historical events.

If at any time you need to take a "time out to get a breath of fresh air" and leave the classroom, or stop the assigned activity or homework, please do so. We ask that you freewrite about what happened — your feelings, your thoughts, what triggered your reaction and why, so you can stabilize them on paper. You will be asked to turn in one copy of your writing.

Appendix A

Confidentiality

Confidentiality belongs to all participants individually, and as a group. Communications from participants will be treated with professional confidence, and reasonable precautions will be taken to protect confidential information obtained through or stored in any medium. These precautions include an awareness of the limited confidentiality guarantees of electronic communication.

The integrity and welfare of all persons, and the information about them that has been obtained in the course of these sessions will be safeguarded. Results of these sessions may be used for teaching, research, publications, or presentations at seminars, conferences and workshops. If your individual results are discussed, your identity will be protected by changing your name and other identifying information. Any information you share in the context of this program will be held in the strictest confidence.

Confidential information provided by participants will not be disclosed to anyone, except as mandated by law to prevent a clear and immediate danger that is life-threatening or could result in serious bodily harm to an individual or to report child abuse, elder abuse, or neglect.

Video or audio records

At the end of this consent form, you will be given the option of allowing us to take photographs and/or make audio or videotape recordings of you which may be used in analyzing the data or in publications and presentations. We may publish and present photographs, audio recordings, and videos of you including your face. No other personal information about you will be included in the presentation.

Participants' Rights

You will not be paid for your participation in this program. Your participation is voluntary, and you are free to withdraw at any time.

You are free to choose not to answer particular questions or participate in particular activities.

Consent Form

Any information developed during the course of the program that may affect your willingness to continue will be provided to you.

If you decide to withdraw, you will be asked to state in writing your reasons for withdrawing for future planning purposes. You will also be asked if the coursework already collected can be used.

Contact Person

If you have any questions about this program, or if concerns arise as a result of working with the materials at home or after class, you may call [insert your contact information].

Consent: Please initial at the beginning of each line.

___I have read this form, and the dissertation/project has been explained to me. I have been given the opportunity to ask questions, and my questions have been answered. If I have additional questions, I have been told whom to contact.

___I agree to participate in the program described above. I will receive a signed copy of this consent form.

___I give permission for photographs or videotapes of me to be used in publications or presentations.

Participant's Name (printed)	Date
Participant's Signature	Date
Witness' Name (printed)	Date
Witness' Signature	Date
Name of person obtaining consent (printed)	Date
Signature of person obtaining consent	Date

Appendix B
Syllabus

Course Description

This course is an exploratory exercise in developing a method to attend to the transgenerational trauma of the transatlantic and domestic slave trade within the context of the African American church community in Virginia. Chattel slavery was designed, developed, and implemented in Virginia. The traumatic impact of chattel slavery on the enslaved Africans and African Americans, and its effect on subsequent generations is the focus of this course. Studies of the Jewish Holocaust, Native American Massacres, the Armenian Genocide, and the African American slave trade describe the intergenerational transmission of trauma, grief, and loss. Healthcare professionals, social scientists, historians, and theologians have identified economic, social, religious, cultural and educational patterns of behavior that are processes perpetuated from generation to generation. This course will engage the results of the research of these disciplines, the history of the transatlantic and domestic slave trade, and the African American Christian religious tradition to develop a method of healing. Using the genogram as an assessment tool, participants will be asked to identify both the positive and negative social, religious, cultural, educational, and economic patterns of their families in order to identify the transgenerational trauma, skills, talents, and resiliency in their families. Participants will also participate in the creation of a generational healing communion ceremony.

Course Objectives

At the end of the program, participants will:

- understand the lasting effects of trauma;
- recognize the importance of family history and how it influences the present;
- appreciate the resiliency of the human spirit and the healing power of faith and prayer;
- design a spiritual discipline to facilitate healing of transgenerational trauma in the African American church community.

Course Requirements

Participants are expected to:

- sign the consent form;
- commit to regular attendance;
- engage in class activities and discussions;
- submit weekly freewriting exercises;
- create a family genogram to identify the trauma, strengths and resilience;
- participate in a healing ceremony;
- bring weekly offerings i.e., items that are personally significant such as prayers, songs, art, music, and writings for the final healing ceremony (all offerings will be returned);
- complete a course evaluation;
- agree to a follow-up gathering or interview within four months.

Course Topics

Session One: The Genogram and Family Systems
Session Two: Old Testament Family Stories
Session Three: Generational Trauma in Jewish, Armenian and Native American History

- Guest Speakers

Appendix B

- Sharing personal stories about generational healing prayer
- Generational Trauma in Jewish, Native American, and Armenian History

Session Four: Generational Trauma in African American History
Session Five: Trauma, Mourning, Resilience, and Hope
Session Six: Evaluation and Healing Service

Session Outline

6:30 p.m.	Opening prayer & video clip
6:40 p.m.	Cinquain exercise
6:50 p.m.	Genogram process check-in
7:00 p.m.	Conversation about previous week's topic or class questions
7:15 p.m.	Offerings
7:30 p.m.	Break
7:40 p.m.	Topic of the week
8:00 p.m.	Freewrite question
8:15 p.m.	Distribute questions for next week
8:20 p.m.	Closing prayer

Guidelines for the Cinquain

A cinquain is a five lined diamond-shaped poem which incorporates oral, analytical thinking, reading, and writing skills.

As part of the opening devotional, the participant will watch and/or listen to material related to the class topics and write a cinquain in response. Once completed, all participants will read their cinquain to the class. Two copies are to be made — one to turn in and one to keep.

Example:

Spider

Furry, black

Climbing, spinning, weaving

They make an intricate web

Tarantula

The formula:

Line 1: Spider	1 NOUN-A
Line 2: Furry, black	2 related ADJECTIVES
Line 3: Climbing, spinning, weaving	3 descriptive GERUNDS (verb + -ing) or a phrase about the title
Line 4: They make an intricate web.	1 complete, related SENTENCE or a feeling about the title—four words
Line 5: Tarantula	1 NOUN-B (a synonym of NOUN-A)

Appendix B

GUIDELINES FOR FREEWRITING

Class participants will be asked to free write as a class activity and assignment. All freewrites are to be edited after completion. Two copies are to be made, one to turn in at the beginning of class and one to keep.

Freewriting—also called stream-of-consciousness writing—is a technique in which a person writes continuously for a set period of time without regard to spelling, grammar, or topic. It produces raw, often unusable material, but helps writers overcome blocks of apathy and self-criticism. It is used mainly by prose writers and writing teachers. Some writers use the technique to collect initial thoughts and ideas on a topic, often as a preliminary to formal writing. Freewriting is not the same as automatic writing. Basic freewriting follows these guidelines:

- Write nonstop for a set period of time (15 minutes).
- Do not make corrections as you write.
- Keep writing, even if you have to write something like, "I don't know what to write."
- Write whatever comes into your mind.
- Do not judge or censor what you are writing.
- Use the writing tool that is most comfortable for you—pencil, computer, or whatever.
- Don't cross anything out: Write the new idea down; leave the old one.
- Drop all punctuation. That can make your freewriting faster and more fluent.

Freewriting is messy. In fact, if your freewriting is neat and coherent, you probably haven't loosened up enough. However, remember that you can't fail in freewriting. The point of doing freewriting is the process, not the end result. At times, a writer may also do focused freewriting letting a chosen topic structure their thoughts. Expanding from this topic, the thoughts may stray to make connections and create more abstract views on the topic. This technique helps a writer explore a particular subject before putting ideas into a more basic context.

Freewriting has these benefits: 1) It makes you more comfortable with the act of writing. 2) It helps you bypass the "inner critic" that can often tell you that you can't write. 3) It can be a valve to release inner tensions. 4) It can help you discover things to write about 5) It can indirectly improve your formal writing.

Resources:
http://web.mst.edu/~gdoty/classes/concepts-practices/free-writing.html
http://en.wikipedia.org/wiki/Free_writing
Peter Elbow—*Writing with Power*
Julia Cameron— *The Artist's Way*

Appendix C

Definitions of Different Trauma Types
(National Child Traumatic Stress Network)

1. Sexual Abuse or Assault

NOTE: If perpetrator is in a caretaking role for youth, event is classified as sexual abuse. Sexual contact/exposure by others (i.e., non-caretakers) is classified as sexual assault/rape.

Actual or attempted sexual contact (e.g., fondling; genital contact; penetration, etc.) and/or exposure to age-inappropriate sexual material or environments (e.g., print, internet or broadcast pornography; witnessing of adult sexual activity) by an adult to a minor child.

Sexual exploitation of a minor child by an adult for the sexual gratification or financial benefit of the perpetrator (e.g., prostitution; pornography; orchestration of sexual contact between two or more minor children).

Unwanted or coercive sexual contact or exposure between two or more minors.

Definitions of Different Trauma Types

2. Physical Abuse or Assault

NOTE: If perpetrator is in a caretaking role for youth, event is classified as physical abuse. Physical contact/exposure by others (i.e., non-caretakers) is classified as physical assault.

Actual or attempted infliction of physical pain (e.g., stabbings; bruising; burns; suffocation) by an adult, another child, or group of children to a minor child with or without use of an object or weapon and including use of severe corporal punishment.

Does not include rough and tumble play or developmentally normative fighting between siblings or peers of similar age and physical capacity (e.g., assault of a physically disabled child by a non-disabled same-aged peer would be included in this category of trauma exposure).

3. Emotional Abuse/Psychological Maltreatment

Acts of commission against a minor child, other than physical or sexual abuse, that caused or could have caused conduct, cognitive, affective or other mental disturbance. These acts include:
   a. Verbal abuse (e.g., insults; debasement; threats of violence)
   b. Emotional abuse (e.g., bullying; terrorizing; coercive control)
   c. Excessive demands on a child's performance (e.g., scholastic; athletic; musical; pageantry) that may lead to negative self-image and disturbed behavior.

Acts of omission against a minor child that caused or could have caused conduct, cognitive, affective or other mental disturbance. These include:
   a. Emotional neglect (e.g., shunning; withdrawal of love)
   b. Intentional social deprivation (e.g., isolation; enforced separation from a parent, caregiver or other close family member)

4. Neglect

Failure by the child victim's caretaker(s) to provide needed, age-appropriate care although financially able to do so, or offered financial or other means to do so. Includes:

a. Physical neglect (e.g., deprivation of food, clothing, shelter)

b. Medical neglect (e.g., failure to provide child victim with access to needed medical or mental health treatments and services; failure to consistently disperse or administer prescribed medications or treatments (e.g., insulin shots)

c. Educational neglect (e.g., withholding child victim from school; failure to attend to special educational needs; truancy)

5. Serious Accident or Illness/Medical Procedure

UNINTENTIONAL injury or accident such as car accident, house fire, serious playground injury, or accidental fall down stairs (accident caused intentionally by another would be classified as Physical Abuse or Assault).

Having a physical illness or experiencing medical procedures that are extremely painful and/or life threatening. Examples of illnesses include AIDS or cancer. Medical procedures include changing burn dressings or undergoing chemotherapy, etc.

6. Witness to Domestic Violence

Exposure to emotional abuse, actual/attempted physical or sexual assault, or aggressive control perpetrated between a parent/caretaker and another adult in the child victim's home environment.

Exposure to any of the above acts perpetrated by an adolescent against one or more adults (e.g., parents, grandparent) in the child victim's home environment.

Definitions of Different Trauma Types

7. Victim/Witness to Community Violence

Extreme violence in the community (i.e., neighborhood violence). Includes exposure to gang-related violence (e.g., drive-by-shootings).

8. School Violence

Violence that occurs in a school setting. It includes, but is not limited to, school shootings, bullying, interpersonal violence among classmates, classmate suicide.

9. Natural or Manmade Disasters

Major accident or disaster that is an unintentional result of a manmade or natural event (e.g., tornado, nuclear reactor explosion).

Does NOT include disasters that are intentionally caused (e.g., Oklahoma City Bombing, bridge collapsing due to intentional damage), which would be classified as acts of terrorism/political violence.

10. Forced Displacement

Forced relocation to a new home due to political reasons. Generally includes political asylees or immigrants fleeing political persecution. Refugees or political asylees who were forced to move and were exposed to war may be classified here and also under war/terrorism/political violence.

11. War/Terrorism/Political Violence

Exposure to acts of war/terrorism/political violence. Includes U.S. incidents such as the Oklahoma City bombing, the 9/11 attacks, or anthrax deaths. Includes incidents outside of the U.S. such as bombing, shooting, looting, or accidents that are a result of terrorist activity (e.g., bridge collapsing due to intentional damage, hostages who are injured during captivity). Includes actions of individuals acting in isolation (i.e., sniper attacks, school shootings) if they are considered political in nature.

APPENDIX C

12. Victim/Witness to Extreme Personal/Interpersonal Violence

Includes extreme violence by or between individuals that has not been reported elsewhere (hence, if the child witnessed domestic violence, this should be recorded as Witness to Domestic Violence and NOT repeated here).

Intended to include exposure to homicide, suicide and other similar extreme events.

13. Traumatic Grief/Separation

Death of a parent, primary caretaker or sibling.

Abrupt, unexpected, accidental or premature death or homicide of a close friend, family member, or other close relative.

Abrupt, unexplained and/or indefinite separation from a parent, primary caretaker, or sibling due to circumstances beyond the child victim's control (e.g., contentious divorce, parental incarceration, or parental hospitalization). Does not include placement in foster care.

14. System-Induced Trauma

Traumatic removal from the home, traumatic foster placement, sibling separation, or multiple placements in a short amount of time.

Appendix D

Program Evaluation

1. My overall evaluation of the course is:

    ☐ Excellent

    ☐ Good

    ☐ Fair

    ☐ Poor

2. Circle "yes" or "no" for the following items:

a. Did the program meet your expectations?	YES	NO
b. Would you recommend this course to a colleague?	YES	NO
c. Was the content of this course relevant?	YES	NO
d. Was there enough time for discussion and questions?	YES	NO

3. To what extent did the program meet the objectives?

    ☐ Completely

    ☐ Much of it

    ☐ Only some of it

    ☐ Not at all

APPENDIX D

4. Can you introduce concepts learned during the class into your family?
   ☐ Yes
   ☐ Much of it
   ☐ Only some of it
   ☐ Not at all

If not at all, why not?

_____

_____

_____

_____

Program Evaluation

Using the scale below, please circle your responses to questions five through seven.

Excellent	Good	Average	Below Average	Poor
5	4	3	2	1

5. Overall quality of the presentations:

   a. Clarity of presentations   5   4   3   2   1
   b. Material related to problems and issues   5   4   3   2   1
   c. Questions and discussions   5   4   3   2   1
   d. Case studies and exercises   5   4   3   2   1
   e. Audio-visual aids   5   4   3   2   1
   f. Additional comments

   _____

   _____

6. Overall quality of facilities:

   a. Instructional facilities   5   4   3   2   1
   b. Meals/breaks   5   4   3   2   1
   c. Parking   5   4   3   2   1
   d. Additional comments

   _____

   _____

7. Please rate the presenters.

   Name of Presenter_____

   a. Well-prepared   5   4   3   2   1

Appendix D

   b. Knowledgeable   5   4   3   2   1
   c. Enthusiastic   5   4   3   2   1
   d. Easy to Understand   5   4   3   2   1
   e. Additional comments

_____

_____

Name of Presenter_____

   a. Well-prepared   5   4   3   2   1
   b. Knowledgeable   5   4   3   2   1
   c. Enthusiastic   5   4   3   2   1
   d. Easy to Understand   5   4   3   2   1
   e. Additional comments

_____

_____

Name of Presenter_____

   a. Well-prepared   5   4   3   2   1
   b. Knowledgeable   5   4   3   2   1
   c. Enthusiastic   5   4   3   2   1
   d. Easy to Understand   5   4   3   2   1
   e. Additional comments

_____

_____

Program Evaluation

Name of Presenter_____

a. Well-prepared	5	4	3	2	1
b. Knowledgeable	5	4	3	2	1
c. Enthusiastic	5	4	3	2	1
d. Easy to Understand	5	4	3	2	1

e. Additional comments

_____

_____

8. What additional information would have been helpful?

_____

_____

9. What did you like best about the course?

_____

_____

10. What did you like least about the class?

_____

_____

Appendix D

11. What issues should have been covered that were not?

_____

_____

12. Do you have any ideas or general comments for future sessions?

_____

_____

13. Do you have any friends, family or colleagues who would benefit from this program?

If yes, may we have their names and contact information?

_____

_____

14. If you were leading this course, what would you add, change, remove?

_____

_____

Thank you for participating!

Appendix E

Roots Matter Healing Service

Welcome and Purpose

We have traveled some stony roads this past six weeks uncovering and discovering things that delight us and disturb us. Things that have overwhelmed us and affirmed us about ourselves our families and our community. Now we come together to lament the suffering of our ancestors, to testify to their resilience and to pray for the healing unresolved historical trauma that we carry so that our children and future generations will be freer to live healthier fruitful lives.

Invocation and Opening Prayer

Loving God,
Pour out your Holy Spirit upon us and grant us
A new vision of your glory
A new experience of your power
A new faithfulness of your word
A new consecration to your service
So that your love may grow in us
And your kingdom come among us
In Jesus name we pray. Amen.

Appendix E

Healing History

Leader: When there is no way forward, when the future is cut off and death is winning, hope can appear unexpectedly, and the universe expands in unthinkable ways. Before hope can appear, survivors of disaster have to find language to tell of it; they have to grieve accumulations of loss and begin to place the catastrophe into larger frames of meaning. After disaster, hope needs space in which to take root, a fallowing of the land, a turning of the soil to aerate and open it. That is the place of the lament to express the feelings of being sinned against. Jesus lamented on the cross when he said "My God, My God why have you forsaken me? He created a space for hope to take root. This is the time for us to lament, to create the space for hope. As we prepare to share our lamentations listen to the lament of our ancestors.

Music:	"Motherless Chile"—Sweet Honey in the Rock
Lamentations:	Class Participants
Refrain:	"My God, My God why have you forsaken me?"

Unison: We lament for those who were captured and the families they were taken from, we weep for those who lived and died on the march to the slave dungeons, for those who lived and died in the slave dungeons and on the slave ships. We cry for those who were lynched, raped, physically and sexually abused, separated from their families and for the broken relationships, we mourn for those who witnessed violence, for those who were cheated out of their jobs, homes and land, for those who were unfairly incarcerated. For those who were mentally ill, who were fearful and anxious. For those who carried and still carry the trauma of their people. Descend upon our hearts, O God, for our wills are weak, our spirits are dry, our bodies are tired, our emotions are bruised. Hear us O God, save us, heal us, and give us hope. Amen.

Honoring Heritage

Leader: "When God had made The Man [and Woman], God made them out of stuff that sung all the time and glittered all over. Then after that, some angels got jealous and chopped them into millions of pieces, but still they glittered and hummed. So those angels beat them down to nothing but sparks, but each little spark had a shine and a song. So those angels covered each one over with mud. And the lonesomeness in the sparks made them hunt for one another, but the mud was deaf and dumb. Like all the other tumbling mud-balls, Janie had tried to show her shine." Zora Neale Hurston—*Their Eyes were Watching God (adapted)*

Our ancestors showed their shine through their gifts and talents in spite of the obstacles they had to face. They were creative in how they protected us from the brutality of racism, sexism, classism and all the other isms. As we prepare to share our shine meditate on this song:

Music: "I Will Give Thanks"—Eli Wilson
Testimonies of Blessing: Class Participants
Refrain: "We are the light of the world, we're gonna let it shine."

Unison: For all the blessings that have been given to our families, we ask for an increase. The gifts of faith, the love of life, the love of education, the value of hard work, the entrepreneurial spirit, the compassion for the least of these, the passion for our children, the respect for the body, the gifts of creating through wood, paint, music, dance. The passion for justice and fairness, the compassion for the elderly, the commitment to our community. The respect for our environment. The gift of persistence and perseverance. And for the blessings yet to be realized, open our eyes to see them, give us the resources to nurture them and show us how to use them. Amen.

Renewing Hope

Leader: In the story of the Gerasene demonic in Mark chapter 5, Jesus encounters a man who has been living in the cemetery. According to scripture, he was possessed by an evil spirit and nobody could keep him tied up with chains. He was too strong for anyone to control. He wandered among the tombs and hills screaming and crying and cutting himself. When he saw Jesus he ran to him. Jesus asked him his name and he responded, my name is mob; there are so many of us. Tormented by memories, trapped in the past like the man in the graveyard we live in our own emotional cemeteries. We are bound with the chains of unhealed memories and unforgiveness. The cure from some of our failings does not always depend altogether on our willpower. There are times when no matter how hard we try some things

APPENDIX E

never change. Only Jesus can give us the peace, the peace that transcends all understanding. Intercessory healing prayer is bringing to light past hurts and asking healing from the wounds in the present. Imagine yourself like the Gerasene demoniac, kneeling before Jesus as you intercede for your family and community.

Music:	"Intercession"—Eli Wilson
Intercessory Prayers:	Class Participants
Refrain:	"My name is mob there are so many of us"
Litany of Intercession:	"For My People"—Margaret Walker (each person read a stanza)

Unison: Almighty God, only you know all our wounds and pain, the extent of suffering that we endure from the trauma of our history. For whatever part we have caused by our actions, consciously or unconsciously we ask your forgiveness. We ask you to heal our hearts.

Help us now and heal our families. Let any hurt or brokenness that has been transmitted through the generations from the trauma of chattel slavery now be healed by your love and your power. We ask Lord that you place your cross between each generation past, present and future, filtering out and cleansing with your blood the pain and trauma from the bloodlines of each generation. We pray to you Jesus to heal their broken hearts, open their eyes and set them free.

Holy God, thank you for sharing with us the wonderful ministry of intercession. Thank for the healing that has happened, is happening and will happen. Lord, cleanse us of any sadness and negative thinking or despair that we may have picked up during this time of intercession. We bind any spirits that are not of you and send them to you to do with what you will. Come Holy Spirit, renew us and fill us anew with your power, your life and your joy. Strengthen us where we feel weak and clothe us with your light, fill us with your life. In Jesus Name we pray. Amen.

Reflection

Invitation to the Table

One: Universal God: From the soil of the earth, you have formed us in your image.
All: Creator God: You brought life out of chaos and began the great act of salvation.

One: Provider God: You fed us manna and quail in the desert, bread and fish with leftovers at the seaside. By your Word, you fed us the bread of life and offered us living water.
All: Compassionate God: You loved us so much that you sent your Son to walk among, suffer with us and die for us.

Unison: Healing God: Through this simple meal, renew our minds, reframe our thoughts, and reorient our hearts to beat with the rhythm of your call to reconciliation and healing of ourselves, our families and our community. Amen.

Words of Institution

On the night before his death, as Jesus took bread among his friends, after giving thanks, he blessed it and broke it. He gave it to his disciples, saying: "Take, eat. This is my body captured, forced marched, placed in the slave dungeon and the slave ship, auctioned, beaten, mutilated, raped, humiliated, interrogated, legislated, silenced, interred, relocated, exiled, excluded, and executed. This is my body, given for you. Do this and remember me."

In the same way, he took a cup and passed it among his friends, saying: "This is the cup of a new covenant, sealed in my blood. Blood shed for the whips, the rapes, the mutilations, the branding. Blood that carries a story of love accumulated and passed backward and forward through generations. Blood that flows with compassion, forgiveness and healing. Whenever you drink it, do this and remember me." Amen.

Whenever you eat of this bread and drink of this cup, you declare my life, my death and my resurrection until I come . . .

Appendix E

Closing Prayer

Unison: We thank you, O God, that you have given us your Son, who is the food of eternal life. Strengthen us, and heal us so that our daily living may be a testimony to your love, grace and power. Amen.

Benediction

"As We Move Deeper"—Mark Nepo

Glossary

Bowen Family System Theory—a theory of human behavior wherein the family is viewed as an emotional unit because of the complex connectedness, reactivity and interdependence of the family members.

Chattel Slavery—an immoral economic system under which human beings are treated as property and held against their will from the time of their capture, purchase or birth, and deprived of the right to leave, to refuse to work, or to demand compensation.

Commemoration—a ceremony or celebration in which a person or event is remembered.

Commemorative (adjective) acting as a memorial or mark of an event or person: a commemorative plaque; (noun) an object such as a stamp or coin made to mark an event or honor a person.

Cultural Heritage—the legacy of physical artifacts (cultural property) and intangible attributes of a group or society that are inherited from past generations, maintained in the present and bestowed for the benefit of future generations. Cultural heritage includes tangible culture (such as buildings, monuments, landscapes, books, works of art, and artifacts), intangible culture (such as folklore, traditions, language, and knowledge), and natural heritage (including culturally-significant landscapes, and biodiversity).

Culture—is that complex whole which includes knowledge, belief, art, morals, law, custom, and any other capabilities and habits acquired by humankind as a member of society.

Glossary

Differentiation of Self—single out one's personhood from the group by drawing distinctions between self and others because there is an innate desire to become authentic individuals.

Disenfranchised Grief—a loss, disappointment or misfortune wherein persons experience a feeling of deep distress and sorrow because the grief is not or cannot be openly acknowledged, socially sanctioned or publicly mourned.

Emotional Trauma—intense irrational feelings wherein a person experiences fear, anxiety, depression, hopelessness as a result of memories of extraordinary stressful events.

Faith—the ability to trust, hope, and believe in goodness, trustworthiness or reliability of God when questions and circumstances cannot be settled by evidence or present experience, in order to thrive under extreme, ongoing pressure without acting in dysfunctional or harmful ways.

Family—a group of people wherein they acknowledge a relationship whether it is perceived positive or negative because they are related to one another by blood, marriage, or cultural tradition (fictive kinship).

Family System—the manner in which family members function in relationship to each other wherein they develop patterns of behavior that are caused by or cause other family members behavior in predictable ways.

Fictive Kinship—a group of people wherein they acknowledge social ties and relationships that are not necessarily predicated on blood ties or marriage ties because they may be based on shared residence, shared economic ties, nurture kinship or familiarity through other forms of interaction.

Generation—a set of persons related by blood or marriage wherein they are regarded as a single step or stage in descent due to being born and living at the same time, growing up becoming adults and having children of their own.

GLOSSARY

Genogram—a pictorial display wherein physical, psychological, spiritual, behavioral, and hereditary patterns are visualized and identified because of a systemic method of recording family history and relationships.

Grief—the emotion felt by person (or animal) when loss occurs.

Heal—cause to become healthy or sound again; alleviate a person's distress or anger; correct or put right.

Healing—the alleviation of or relief from pain and brokenness wherein a person experiences therapeutic, medicinal, and/or spiritual health-giving restoration due to curative treatment and repair.

Healing Prayer—the alleviation of pain and brokenness wherein persons experience freedom from the effects of mental, spiritual, and physical injury and trauma because of the presence of Jesus Christ through the ministry of the Holy Spirit.

Historical Trauma (HT)—is cumulative emotional and psychological wounding, over the lifespan and across generations, emanating from violence inflicted on a large group of people. Historical trauma is an example of how intergenerational pain experienced by an individual in an earlier generation can have effects that reach into the lives of future generations. For example, a pattern of maternal abandonment of a child at a young age might be seen across three generations. (Maria Yellow Horse Brave Heart www.historicaltrauma.com)

Historical Trauma Response (HTR)—is a constellation of features in reaction to these abusive life events. The HTR may include substance abuse as a vehicle for attempting to numb the pain associated with the emotional upheaval. The HTR often includes other types of self-destructive behavior, suicidal thoughts and gestures, depression, anxiety, low self-esteem, anger, and difficulty recognizing and expressing emotions. Associated with HTR is historical unresolved grief. (Maria Yellow Horse Brave Heart www.historicaltrauma.com)

History—the study of past events wherein information is discovered, collected, organized and presented in order to investigate patterns of cause

Glossary

and effect or providing a perspective; the discovery, collection, organization, and presentation of information about past events.

Hope—the expectation, anticipation, wish, longing for, dreaming of justice, equality, fairness in order to create wholeness, freedom, healing, peace, and well-being.

Imago Dei—the Christian doctrine wherein it is believed that the human being, by virtue of Jesus Christ, possesses a divinely-bestowed dignity (the image of God) in order to become actively engaged in his or her part in Christ's mission and his or her own spiritual pilgrimage.

Intercession—the action of intervening on behalf of another person, by talking to God for healing, awareness of God's peace, power, presence in reinforcing the interconnectedness of humankind.

Intercessory Prayer—the action of saying a prayer on behalf of another person.

Loss—the absence of something perceived to be of value wherein a person (or animal) experiences sadness and sorrow.

Memory—a conscious and unconscious collection of information and experiences wherein an organism in the person encodes, stores, and recalls data in order to evaluate, interact, and communicate with her/his environment.

Mental Trauma—frightening thoughts wherein a sense of helplessness, vulnerability, and danger occurs as a result of extraordinary stressful events, e.g., war, terrorism, earthquake, rape or long term abuse; racism, sexual abuse, chronic illness, poverty. Example: someone is out to get me . . . police are dangerous.

Multigenerational—of or relating to more than one generation wherein interactions and relationships are established among members of generations because of family, social, vocational, economic, cultural, or faith traditions.

Pastoral Counseling—assistance and guidance within the context of a religious faith tradition in order to resolve, heal or transform personal, spiritual, social or psychological problems or difficulties.

Physical Trauma—psychosomatic distress as a result of brutal force (injury) to the human body (e.g., domestic violence, bullying, combat) or stress-related, stress-induced life experiences (e.g., heart disease, diabetes, cancer) or neurological changes to the brain and brain chemistry because of drugs and substance abuse.

Redemption—a Christian theological concept of being saved from sin, error or evil whereby surrendering one's life, will, ego to Jesus Christ in order to gain healing and wholeness.

Remember—the ability to bring to one's mind an awareness of someone or something that one has seen, known or experienced in the past; wherein the person responds with actions or thoughts or behaviors in order to share and exchange information, convey and transmit feelings and emotions, or make an idea, impression or consciousness known.

Resilience—the ability to adapt to difficult or challenging life experiences wherein a person overcomes adversity, recovers from disruptive change or misfortune in order to thrive under extreme, on-going pressure without acting in dysfunctional or harmful ways.

Resistance—the refusal to accept or comply with persons, situations or institutions wherein a person attempts to prevent by action or argument in order to oppose legal, political, economic, social, and spiritual injustice.

Secret—knowledge or information withheld by a person or group of persons from others because of shame, trauma, perceived danger or desire to control.

Slavery—institution based on a relationship of dominance and submission, whereby one person owns another and can exact from that person labor or other services against their will.

Glossary

Suffering—the result of trauma wherein a person experiences dysfunctional behavior, emotional upheaval, false beliefs, distress, affliction, stress, and misery due to unprocessed wounding and grief.

Tragedy—a negative disruptive event wherein a person experiences great suffering destruction or distress because of a serious accident, illness, crime, natural disaster, betrayal, deception, injustice or ethical dilemma.

Transgenerational—of or relating to an event or experience wherein beliefs and behaviors are passed on to subsequent generations because of family narratives, rituals, imagery and symbolism.

Trauma—a psychophysical experience of serious threat and/or injury wherein frightening thoughts, painful emotions and physical distress occur due to acts of abandonment, aggression, betrayal, stressful events or long term duress.

Triangle—an emotional attachment relationship involving usually three persons, but may have a surrogate person/entity in the form of a career, hobby, ministry etc., wherein the relationship can be stabilized by shifting tension around the three relationships.

Wholeness—the state of being, in which a person is unbroken, undamaged or restored, repaired; wherein their identity is complete because they have the ability to relate to others in a life giving manner.

Bibliography

Apprey, Maurice. "The African-American Experience: Forced Immigration and Transgenerational Trauma." *Mind and Human Interaction* 4 (1993) 70–75.

———. "Reinventing the Self in the Face of Received Transgenerational Hatred in the African American Community." *Journal of Applied Psychoanalytic Studies* 1/2 (1999) 131–43.

——— "Staging and Transforming Historical Grievances: From Cultural Memory to a Reconstructable Future." *Journal for the Psychoanalysis of Culture and Society* 3.1 (1998) 81–90.

Battle, Michael. *Reconciliation: The Ubuntu Theology of Desmond Tutu*. Cleveland: Pilgrim, 1997.

———. *Ubuntu: I in You and You in Me*. New York: Seabury, 1984.

Becvar, Dorothy. *In the Presence of Grief: Helping Family Members Resolve Death, Dying and Bereavement Issues*. New York: Guildford, 2001.

Bediako, Kwame. *Jesus in Africa: The Christian Gospel in African History and Experience*. Waynesboro, GA: Paternoster, 2000.

Berenbaum, Michael. *The World Must Know: The History of the Holocaust as Told in the United States Holocaust Memorial Museum*. Baltimore: Johns Hopkins University Press, 2005.

Berlin, Ira. *Many Thousands Gone: the First Two Centuries of Slavery in North America*. Cambridge, MA: Belknap, 2000.

Bloom, Sandra L. *Creating Sanctuary: Toward the Evolution of Sane Societies*. New York: Routledge, 1997.

Bloom, Sandra L., and M. Reichert. *Bearing Witness: Violence and Collective Responsibility*. Binghamton, NY: Haworth, 1998.

The Bowen Center. "Differentiation of Self." https://www.thebowencenter.org/theory/eight-concepts/differentiation-of-self/.

———. "Multigenerational Transmission Process." https://www.thebowencenter.org/theory/eight-concepts/multigenerational-transmission-process/.

———. "Theory." https://www.thebowencenter.org/theory/.

Boyajian, K., and Grigorian, H. "Sequelae of the Armenian Genocide on Survivors." Paper presented at the International Conference on the Holocaust and Genocide, Tel Aviv, Israel, June 20–24, 1982.

———. "Psychological Sequelae of the Armenian Genocide." In *The Armenian Genocide in Perspective*, edited by R. G. Hovannisian, 177–85. New Brunswick, NJ: Transaction, 1988.

Bibliography

Boyd-Franklin, Nancy. *Black Families in Therapy.* New York: Guildford, 1989.

Brave Heart, Maria Yellow Horse. "The Impact of Historical Trauma: The Example of the Native Community." In *Trauma Transformed: An Empowerment UVAResponses*, edited by M. Bussey and J. Wise, 176–93. New York: Columbia University Press, 2007.

———. "Wakiksuyapi: Carrying the Historical Trauma of the Lakota." *Tulane Studies in Social Welfare* 21–22 (2000) 245–66.

Brave Heart, Maria Yellow Horse, and Lemyra M. DeBruyn. "The American Indian Holocaust: Healing Historical Unresolved Grief." *The Journal of the National Center American Indian and Alaska Native Programs* 8/2 (1998) 56–78.

Butterfield, F. *All God's Children: The Bosket Family and the American Tradition of Violence.* New York: Knopf, 1995.

Campbell, Benjamin. *Richmond's Unhealed History.* Richmond, VA: Brandylane, 2011.

Cannon, Katie Geneva. "Cutting Edge Christian Imperialism and the Transatlantic Slave Trade." *Journal of Feminist Studies* 24/1 (2008) 127–34.

———. "An Ethical Mapping of the Transatlantic Slave Trade." In *Religion and Poverty: Pan-African Perspectives*, edited by Peter J. Paris, 19–38. Durham: Duke University Press, 2009.

———. *Katie's Canon: Womanism and the Soul of the Black Community.* New York: Continuum, 1995.

———. "Racism and Economics: The Perspective of Oliver Cox." In *Womanist Theological Ethics: A Reader*, edited by Katie Geneva Cannon, Emilie M. Townes, and Angela D. Sims, 3–20. Louisville: Westminster John Knox, 2011.

Cannon, Katie Geneva, Emilie Townes, and Angela Sim, eds. *Womanist Theological Ethics: A Reader.* Louisville: Westminster John Knox, 2011.

Carter, Harold. *The Prayer Tradition of Black People.* Baltimore: Gateway, 1976.

Chavis, Annie McCullough. "Genograms and African American Families: Employing Family Strengths, Religion, and Extended Family Networks." *Michigan Family Review* 9/1 (2004) 30–36.

Cloud, H., and J. Townsend. *Secrets of Your Family Tree: Healing for Adult Children of Dysfunctional Families.* Chicago: Moody Bible Institute, 1995.

Coleman, Monica. *Making a Way Out of No Way: A Womanist Theology.* Innovations: African American Religious Thought. Minneapolis: Fortress, 2008.

Coleman, Will. *Tribal Talk: Black Theology, Hermeneutics, and African/American Ways of "Telling the Story."* University Park: Pennsylvania State University Press, 2000.

Cone, James. *The Cross and the Lynching Tree.* Maryknoll, NY: Orbis, 2011.

Cooper-Lewter, Nicholas, and Henry Mitchell. *Soul Theology: The Heart of Black Culture.* Nashville: Abingdon, 1986.

Cross, June. *This Far by Faith: African American Spiritual Journeys.* DVD. Disc 3. Directed by Dante James. Alexandria, VA: PBS Video, 2003.

Cugoano, Ouobna Ottobah. *Narrative of the Enslavement of Ottobah Cugoano, a Native of Africa, Published by Himself, in the Year 1787.* Chapel Hill: University of North Carolina Press, 1999. http://www.docsouth.unc.edu/neh/cugoano/cugoano.html.

Danieli, Yael, ed. *International Handbook of Multigenerational Legacies of Trauma.* New York: Plenum, 1998.

Davies, Norman, and Richard Lukas. *The Forgotten Holocaust: The Poles under German Occupation, 1939–1944.* New York: Hippocrene, 2001.

BIBLIOGRAPHY

Davis, David Brion. *In the Image of God: Religion, Moral Values, and Our Heritage of Slavery*. New Haven: Yale University Press, 2001.

———. *Slavery in the Colonial Chesapeake*. Williamsburg, VA: Colonial Williamsburg Foundation, 1986.

Dearing, Norma. *The Healing Touch: A Guide to Healing Prayers for Yourself and Those You Love*. Grand Rapids: Chosen, 2002.

DeGruy Leary, Joy. *Post Traumatic Slave Syndrome: America's Legacy of Enduring Injury and Healing*. Milwaukee: Uptone, 2005.

Dubois, W. E. B. *Prayers for Dark People*. Amherst: University of Massachusetts Press, 1980.

Dubois, W. E. B., Booker T. Washington, and James W. Johnson. *Three Negro Classics: Up From Slavery, The Souls of Black Folks, The Autobiography of an Ex-Colored Man*. New York: Avon, 1965.

Eck, Werner. "The Bar Kokhba Revolt: The Roman Point of View." *The Journal of Roman Studies* 89 (1999) 76–89. http://www.jstor.org/stable/300735.

Eltis, David, and Martin Halbert. "The Transatlantic Slave Trade Data Base." Slave Voyages. http://www.slavevoyages.org.

Eltis, David, and David Richardson. *Atlas of the Transatlantic Slave Trade*. Lewis Walpole Series in Eighteenth-Century Culture and History. New Haven: Yale University Press, 2010.

Eyerman, Ron. "The Past in the Present: Culture and the Transmission of Memory." *Acta Sociologica* 47/2 (2004) 159–69. http://www.jstor.org/stable/4195021.

Fayer, Steve. *Africans in America: America's Journey through Slavery*. DVD. Disc 1–2. Directed by Noland Walker, Jacquie Jones, and Susan Bell. South Burlington, VT: WGBH Boston, 2000.

Fleischner, Jennifer B. *Mastering Slavery: Memory, Family, and Identity in Women's Slave Narratives*. New York: NYU Press, 1996.

Foner, E. *Nothing But Freedom: Emancipation and Its Legacy*. Baton Rouge: Louisiana State University Press, 2007.

Foster, Richard. *Prayer: Finding the Heart's True Home*. San Francisco: Harper, 1992.

Fosu, Kwaku Amoako-Attah. *Handbook on Kente Designs and Adinkra Symbols*. Kumasi, Ghana: Amok, 2007.

Franklin, John Hope, and Evelyn Higginbotham. *From Slavery to Freedom: A History of African Americans*. 9th ed. New York: McGraw-Hill, 2011.

Galindo, Israel. *A Family Genogram Workbook*. Richmond, VA: Educational Consultants, 2006.

Gates, Henry Louis. *Unchained Memories: Readings from the Slave Narratives*. Boston: Bulfinch, 2003.

Gil, Eliana. *The Healing Power of Play: Working with Abused Children*. New York: Guildford, 1991.

Harms, R. *The Diligent: A Voyage through the Worlds of the Slave Trade*. New York: Basic Books, 2002.

Harris, Mark Jonathan. *Unchained Memories: Readings from the Slave Narratives*. DVD. Directed by Ed Bell and Thomas Lenamin. Burbank, CA: Time Warner, 2003.

Hedgepeth, Sonja, and Rochelle Saidel. *Sexual Violence against Jewish Women during the Holocaust*. Lebanon, NH: University Press of New England, 2010.

Herman, Judith. *Trauma and Recovery: The Aftermath of Violence—from Domestic Abuse to Political Terror*. NewYork: Basic Books, 1997.

Bibliography

Herron, Carolivia. *Thereafter Johnnie.* Fairfield, CA: First Book, 2001.

Hintze, Rebecca. *Healing Your Family History: 5 Steps to Break Free of Destructive Patterns.* California: Hay House, 2006.

Hodge, Dwight. R. *Spiritual Assessment: Handbook for Helping Professionals.* Botsford, CT: North American Association of Christians in Social Work, 2003.

———. "Spiritual Eco-maps: a New Diagrammatic Tool for Assessing Marital and Family Spirituality." *Journal of Marital and Family Therapy* 26/1 (2002) 229–40.

Jacobs, Harriet. *Incidents in the Life of a Slave Girl.* Mineola, NY: Dover, 2001.

Janoff-Bulman, J. *Shattered Assumptions: Toward a New Psychology of Trauma.* New York: Free Press, 1992.

Johnson, Matthew. "The Middle Passage, Trauma and the Tragic Re-Imagination of African American Theology." *Pastoral Psychology* 53/6 (2005) 541–61.

———. *The Tragic Vision of African American Religion.* New York: Palgrave, 2010.

Jones, Laura K., and Jenny L. Cureton. "Trauma Redefined in the DSM-5: Rationale and Implications for Counseling Practice." *The Professional Counselor* 4/3 (2014) 257–71. http://tpcjournal.nbcc.org/trauma-redefined-in-the-dsm-5-rationale-and-implications-for-counseling-practice/.

Judy, Dwight. *Christian Meditation and Inner Healing.* Sulpher Spring, WV: OSL, 2010.

Karr-Morse, Robin, and Meredith S. Wiley. *Ghosts from the Nursery: Tracing Roots of Violence.* New York: Atlantic Monthly, 1997.

Kaufman, Jeffrey. *Loss of the Assumptive World: A Theory of Traumatic Loss.* New York: Brounner and Routledge, 2002.

Kerr, Michael E. "One Family's Story: A Primer on Bowen Theory." The Bowen Center for the Study of the Family. 2000. http://www.thebowencenter.org.

Keshgegian, Flora A. *Redeeming Memories: A Theology of Healing and Transformation.* Nashville: Abingdon, 2000.

Kiple Kenneth F. *The Caribbean Slave: A Biological History.* Cambridge: Cambridge University Press, 2002.

Klein, Herbert S. *The Atlantic Slave Trade.* 2nd ed. Cambridge: Cambridge University Press, 2010.

Kupelian, Diane, Anie Sanentz Kalayjian, and Alice Kassabian. "The Turkish Genocide of the Armenians: Continuing Effects on Survivors and Their Families Eight Decades after Massive Trauma." In *International Handbook of Multigenerational Legacies of Trauma,* edited by Yael Danieli, 191–210. New York: Plenum, 1998.

LeSourd, Leonard E. *Touching the Heart of God on Behalf of Others.* Old Tappan, NJ: Chosen, 1990.

Lindqvist, Sven. *Exterminate All The Brutes.* New York: The New Press, 2007

MacNutt, Francis. *Prayer That Heals: Praying for Healing in the Family.* Notre Dame, IN: Ave Maria, 2005.

Marlin, E. *Genograms: The New Tool for Exploring the Personality, Career and Love Patterns You Inherit.* Chicago: Contemporary, 1989.

McAll, Kenneth. *Healing the Family Tree.* London: Sheldon, 1986.

McCoy-Wilson, Sonya Lynette. "Transgenerational Ghosting in the Psyches and Somas of African Americans and their Literatures." MA thesis, Georgia State University, 2008. http://scholarworks.gsu.edu/english_theses/39/.

McGoldrick, Monica. *Genograms: Assessment and Intervention.* New York: Norton, 2008.

———. *Revisioning Family Therapy: Race Culture and Gender in Clinical Practice.* New York: Guildford, 2008.

Bibliography

McGoldrick, Monica, Randy Gerson, and Sueli Petry. *Genograms: Assessment and Intervention*. 3rd ed. New York: Norton, 2008.

Morrison, Toni. *Beloved*. New York: Random House, 2004.

Moss, Donald. *Hating in the First Person Plural: Psychoanalytic Essays on Racism, Homophobia, Misogyny, and Terror*. New York: Other, 2003.

Murray, Andrew. *The Ministry of Intercessory Prayer*. Minneapolis: Bethany, 1981.

Newberg, Andrew, Eugene D'Aquili, and Vince Rause. *Why God Won't Go Away: Brain Science and the Biology of Belief*. New York: Ballantine, 2002.

Noel, James, and Matthew Johnson, eds. *The Passion of the Lord: African American Reflections*. Minneapolis: Fortress, 2005.

O'Connor, Kathleen M. *Jeremiah: Pain and Promise*. Minneapolis: Augsburg Fortress, 2011.

Painter, Nell. *Soul Murder and Slavery*. Charles Edmondson Historical Lecture 15. Waco, TX: Baylor University Press, 1995.

Parker, Russ. *Healing Wounded History: Reconciling Peoples and Healing Places*. London: Darton, Longman and Todd, 2001.

———. *Healing Wounded History: The Workbook*. London: Darton, Longman and Todd, 2001.

Payne, John. *The Healing of Individuals, Families and Nations*. Forres, Scotland: Findhorn, 2005.

Pinderhughes, Elaine. "Black Genealogy Revisited: Restorying an African American Family." In *Re-Visioning Family Therapy: Race, Culture and Gender in Clinical Practice*, edited by Monica McGoldrick, 179–99. New York: Guildford, 1998.

———. "The Multigenerational Transmission of Loss and Trauma: The African American Experience." In *Living Beyond Loss: Death in the Family*, edited by Froma Walsh and Monica McGoldrick, 161–81. 2nd ed. New York: Norton, 2004.

———. *Understanding Race, Ethnicity, and Power: the Key to Efficacy in Clinical Practice*. New York: Free Press, 1989.

Powery, Luke A. *Dem Dry Bones: Preaching, Death, and Hope*. Minneapolis: Fortress, 2012.

Rambo, Shelly. "Shelly Rambo: The Space between Death and Resurrection." *Faith and Leadership*, July 28, 2014. https://www.faithandleadership.com/qa/shelly-rambo-the-space-between-death-and-resurrection.

———. *Spirit and Trauma: A Theology of Remaining*. Nashville: Westminster John Knox, 2010.

Richo, David. *The Five Things We Cannot Change: And the Happiness We Find by Embracing Them*. Boston: Shambhala, 2006.

Roberts, Tara. "Ghosts of Relationships." *Essence Magazine* 39/4 (August 2008) 128.

Robinson, Dominic. *Understanding the "Imago Dei": The Thought of Barth, von Balthasar and Moltmann*. Burlington, VT: Ashgate, 2011.

Rodriguez, J., and T. Fortier. *Cultural Memory: Resistance, Faith, and Identity*. Austin: University of Texas Press, 2007.

Rothschild, Babette. *The Body Remembers: The Psychophysiology of Trauma and Trauma Treatment*. New York: Norton, 2000.

Salerian, A. "A Psychological Report: Armenian Genocide Survivors—67 Years Later." Paper presented at the International Conference on the Holocaust and Genocide, Tel Aviv, Israel, June 20–24, 1982.

Bibliography

Scaer, Robert. *The Body Bears the Burden: Trauma, Dissociation and Disease.* New York: The Haworth Medical, 2001.

Schumm, Darla. "A Review of Spirit and Trauma: a Theology of Remaining." *Journal of Religion, Disability and Health* 15/3 (August 2011) 334–35.

Schutzenberger, A. A. *The Ancestor Syndrome: Transgenerational Psychotherapy and the Hidden Links in the Family Tree.* Translated by A. Trager. New York: Routledge, 1998.

Scott, K. Michelle. "A Perennial Mourning: Identity Conflict and the Transgenerational Transmission of Trauma within the African American Community." *Mind and Human Interaction* 1 (Spring 2001) 11–26.

Sears, Robert T., "Healing and Family Spiritual/Emotional Systems." *The Journal of Christian Healing* 5/1 (1983) 10–23.

Shengold, Leonard. *Soul Murder: The Effects of Childhood Abuse and Deprivation.* New York: Ballentine, 1991.

Smith, Archie. *The Relational Self: Ethics and Therapy from a Black Church Perspective.* Nashville: Abingdon, 1997.

Smith, Patricia. *From Generation to Generation: A Manual for Healing.* Jacksonville, FL: Jehovah Rapha, 1996.

Snyder, Timothy. *Bloodlands: Europe Between Hitler and Stalin.* London: Bodley Head, 2010.

Stanley, Alessandra. "A PBS Documentary Makes Its Case for the Armenian Genocide, With or Without a Debate." *New York Times,* April 17, 2006. http://www.nytimes.com/2006/04/17/arts/television/17stan.html?_r=0.

Sullender, Scott. *Grief and Growth: Pastoral Resource for Emotional and Spiritual Growth.* New York: Paulist, 1985.

———. *Losses in Later Life: A New Way of Walking with God.* 2nd ed. Binghamton, NY: Haworth Pastoral, 1999.

Tadman, Michael. *Speculators and Slaves: Masters, Traders, and Slaves in the Old South.* Madison: University of Wisconsin Press, 1996.

Takagi, M. *Rearing Wolves to Our Own Destruction: Slavery in Richmond, Virginia, 1782–1865.* Charlottesville: University of Virginia Press, 1999.

Tauke, Beverly. *Overcoming the Sins of the Family: Becoming the Redemptive Generation.* Carol Stream, IL: Tyndale, 2004.

Thompson, Curt. *Anatomy of the Soul: Surprising Connections between Neuroscience and Spiritual Practices That Can Transform Your Life and Relationships.* Carol Stream, IL: Tyndale, 2010.

Thurman, Howard. *Jesus and the Disinherited.* Boston: Beacon, 1976.

———. *Luminous Darkness: A Personal Anatomy of Segregation and the Ground of Hope.* New York: Harper & Row, 1965.

Trammell, Jack. *The Richmond Slave Trade: The Economic Backbone of the Old Dominion.* Charleston, SC: History Press, 2012.

Tutu, Desmond. *No Future Without Forgiveness.* New York: Image, 2000.

Ulsamer, B. *The Healing Power of the Past: A New Approach to Healing Family Wounds.* Nevada City, CA: Underwood, 2005.

Van der Kolk, Bessel A., Alexander C. McFarlane, and Lars Weisaeth, eds. *Traumatic Stress: The Effects of Overwhelming Experience on Mind, Body and Society.* New York: Guildford, 1996.

Vennard, Jane E. *Praying for Friends and Enemies: Intercessory Prayer.* Minneapolis: Augsburg, 1995.

Volf, Miroslav. *The End of Memory: Remembering Rightly in a Violent World.* Grand Rapids: Eerdmans, 2006.
Walsh, Froma. *Spiritual Resources in Family Therapy.* 2nd ed. New York: Guildford, 2009.
———. *Strengthening Family Resilience.* 2nd ed. New York: Guildford, 2011.
Weingarten, Kaethe. *Common Shock: Witnessing Violence Everyday: How We Are Harmed, How We Can Heal.* New York: Dutton, 2003.
Wilkerson, Isabel. *The Warmth of Other Suns: The Epic Story of America's Great Migration.* Reprint ed. New York: Vintage, 2011.
Williams, Heather Andrea. *Help Me to Find My People: The African American Search for Family Lost in Slavery.* John Hope Franklin Series in African American History and Culture. Chapel Hill: The University of North Carolina Press, 2012.
Williams, T. *Black Pain: It Just Looks Like We're Not Hurting.* New York: Scribner, 2008.
Worthington, Everett. *Forgiveness and Reconciling: Bridges to Wholeness and Hope.* Downers Grove, IL: InterVarsity, 2003.
———. *A Just Forgiveness: Responsible Healing Without Excusing Justice.* Downers Grove, IL: InterVarsity, 2009.
Wytwycky, Bohdan. *The Other Holocaust: Many Circles of Hell.* Washington, DC: Novak Report, 1982.
Yehuda, R., et.al "Phenomenology and Psychobiology of the Intergenerational Response to Trauma." In *International Handbook of Multigenerational Legacies of Trauma*, edited by Yael Danieli, 639–56. New York: Plenum, 1998.
Zinn, Howard. *A People's History of the United States: 1492 to Present.* New York: Harper, 2005.

www.ingramcontent.com/pod-product-compliance
Lightning Source LLC
Chambersburg PA
CBHW070255230426
43664CB00014B/2545